REBEL IRELAND

REBEL IRELAND

Easter Rising to Civil War

SEAN McMAHON

ᛣ ERCIER PRESS

MERCIER PRESS
Douglas Village, Cork
Website: www.mercierpress.ie

Trade enquiries to CMD Distribution
55A Spruce Avenue, Stillorgan Industrial Park
Blackrock, County Dublin
Tel: (01) 294 2560; Fax: (01) 294 2564
E-mail: cmd@columba.ie

Originally published as three books: *The 1916 Rising* [1999],
The War of Independence [2000] and *The Civil War* [2001]

ISBN 1 85635 498 9
10 9 8 7 6 5 4 3 2 1

A CIP record for this title is available from the British Library

Mercier Press receives financial assistance from
the Arts Council/An Chomhairle Ealaíon

Printed and Bound by J. H. Haynes & Co. Ltd, Sparkford

CONTENTS

1

THE RED-GOLD FLAME

I remember once as a boy half-learning a patriotic song called 'Who Fears to Speak of Easter Week?' It was written anonymously by a nun in flattering imitation of 'The Memory of the Dead', the famous Ninety-Eight ballad of John Kells Ingram (1823–1907), and began with the quatrain:

> Who fears to speak of Easter Week?
> Who does its fate deplore?
> The red-gold flame of Ireland's name
> Confronts the world once more!

It was written some time after the executions of the leaders of the Easter Rising perhaps during the Anglo-Irish War of 1919–21, when patriotism for a majority of people, especially outside of Ulster, had become pure and simple.

Both before or after those two-and-a-half years the response to 1916 would have considerably more muddied. The general reaction to the events of Easter Week, as will become clear, was far from enthusiastic throughout the nationalist community. Yet a majority of these people whose reactions varied from rage to hatred would suffer a remarkable change in the weeks and months after Pearse's unconditional surrender at Great Britain Street (as Parnell Street was then called) at 3.30 p.m. on Saturday, 29 April 1916 to Brigadier-General W. H. M. Lowe. Those who had witnessed the drilling and marching with interest or derision for nearly a year were surprised at the outbreak of fighting and many who watched the volunteers march to their imprisonment in the Rotunda grounds in what seemed like ignominy were soon to cease their mockery and become part of the struggle.

Part of the anger shown by the Dublin citizens originated in the fact that many had fathers, brothers, sons and uncles fighting in the Great War in Irish regiments for a number of reasons, mainly economic, a good number believing that their participation in the 'war to end wars' was to be ultimately for the benefit of their own 'small nation'. Such irreproachable patriots as Arthur Griffith (1871–1922), founder of Sinn Féin, Bulmer Hobson (1883–69), writer and member of the Irish Republican Brotherhood (IRB); Thomas Kettle (1880–1916), poet, essayist and nationalist MP; Francis Ledwidge (1887–1917) poet and trades union organiser; Robert Lynd (1879–1949), nationalist journalist, essayist and critic, and friend of James Connolly; John Redmond (1856–1918), the leader of the Home Rule party and his deputy John Dillon (1851–1927) were horrified to hear of the occupation of the GPO, City Hall, Boland's Mills and the other not particularly strategic buildings on Easter Monday, 24 April and felt betrayed that the constitutional and non-violent strategies of the nationalist and Sinn Féin parties which had seemed to successful had been betrayed.

The mixture of dismay and ribaldry that greeted the Rising in the city was muted compared with the general surprise. Yeats' famous poem 'Easter 1916', published in *Michael Robartes and the Dancer* (1922) underscores this mixture of bewilderment and mockery:

> Being certain that they and I
> But lived where motley is worn:
> All changed, changed utterly:
> A terrible beauty is born.

The main reason for the bewilderment was that armed rising was considered a thing of the past; *pace* the enthusiasm of the reverend balladeer, 'the red glow flame of Ireland's name' had barely flickered for more that a century.

The United Irishmen, rising in the summer of 1798, the 'Year of Liberty' with short-lived forays in Antrim, Down, Carlow, Dublin, Mayo and a more effective and longer-lasting insurrection in Wexford was a kind of waking from a long sleep but apart from a kind of limited affray such as Robert Emmet's premature adventure in Dublin in July

1803 the nineteenth century was relatively quiet. The tithe wars of the 1830s and the continuing agrarian outrages of the secret societies though locally bloody did not amount to world-shaking events. The Young Irelanders led by William Smith O'Brien (1803–64) – the 'Middle-Aged Irelander' as he called himself – after the death of Thomas Davis (1814–45) had a risibly unsuccessful and largely bloodless rebellion in 1848 and the Fenians in the 1860s were not much more effective. The Smith O'Brien rising had coincided with the worst year of the Great Famine and the country had changed completely by the time the Fenian Brotherhood were making so much noise in Canada, Manchester and Clerkenwell. Political activity under Isaac Butt (1813–79), Charles Stewart Parnell (1846–91) and John Redmond had been generally constitutional and non-violent, though some of the events of the Land War had been bloody, and aberrations like the murder of Lord Frederick Cavendish, the newly-appointed chief secretary and the under-secretary T. H. Burke, by the Invincibles (an extremist society with Fenian connections) in May 1882 were not unknown.

This sense of inactivity was put succinctly by Roger Casement, one of the significant players in the Rising, in a letter written from Germany to his friend Joe McGarrity of Clan na Gael in April 1915:

> So far the mass of the exponents of Irish nationality have
> contented themselves for over a century with deeds not
> words.

The Fenian movement did, however, generate two organisations which were to play significant parts in events nearly sixty years later: the IRB and Clan na Gael. The second of these was based in America and by 1870 had 10,000 members. It came under the leadership of John Devoy (1842–1928), a Fenian from County Kildare, who after five years of imprisonment had emigrated to America in 1871. He had played an important part in the Land League agitation of the 1880s and was a sponsor of the Easter Rising, which could be considered as an IRB manifestation even if only a fraction of a fraction of its members were involved. Links had been established by the Americans with this generally disorganised association by 1880 and though it was largely inactive during the leadership of Parnell and the Parliamentary Party it had a revival in the first decade of the new century when the vacuum caused by the leader's fall and death (1890–1) was filled with a variety of political movements.

Though there was no significant armed revolt during the nineteenth-century there had nevertheless been generated a revolutionary iconography with its own sacred texts. Ninety-Eight had produced contemporary broadsheet ballads and the columns of *The Nation* (1842–8), the organ of Young Ireland, were filled up with literary ones such as 'The Memory of the Dead' and 'The Croppy Boy' by William McBurney (1844–92). The centenary of 1798 had produced many more. The celebrations at home and in America and Australia had passed off peacefully but the implicit approval of the aims of the revolutionaries and the enthusiastic singing of such ballads as 'Boolavogue' and 'The Boys of Wexford' showed that there was still a sentimental (if safe) attachment to what was for many the 'old cause'. 'Bold Robert Emmet' apart from being the subject of a popular turn-of-the century ballad and the protagonist of a popular 'drama' as played by travelling companies and many amateur societies, had also left a much-quoted 'speech from the dock'.

Most significant in light of later claims was the Fenian oath which was taken by all members of both the IRB and Clan na Gael:

> I do solemnly swear allegiance to the Irish Republic, now virtually established; that I will take up arms at a moment's notice to defend its integrity and independence; that I will yield implicit obedience to the commands of my superior, and finally I take this oath in the spirit of the true soldier of liberty. So help me, God.

The words 'now virtually established' formed the basis for all subsequent claims of paramilitaries that what they were conducting was a war, the authority of the notional republic being the basis for their moral stance.

The tremendous popularity of Lady Gregory's play *The Rising of the Moon* (1907), about the innate nationalism of an RIC sergeant, and of *Cathleen Ni Houlihan*, the 1798 play that Yeats wrote in 1902 for his revolutionary English born love Maud Gonne (both in their time members of the IRB) showed that there was a living tradition which did not look unkindly on past rebellions, whatever their feelings about a twentieth-century one. Stephen Gwynn (1864–1950), the Protestant nationalist MP and grandson of Smith O'Brien, wrote after seeing Maud Gonne in the play, 'I went home asking myself if such plays should be produced unless one was prepared to go out and shoot and be shot.' Yeats too wondered in the year of his death:

> Did that play of mine send out
> Certain men the English shot?

Apart from the raising of nationalist awareness brought about by the centenary and the conscious Irishness of the Literary Revival there were also in existence two overtly non-political institutions that played a similar part in the rise of the 'new nationalism'. These were the Gaelic Athletic Association and the Gaelic League and both were deliberate asserters of non-English Irishness. The first, begun in 1884 by Michael Cusack (1847–1906), may very well have been a deliberate initiative by the Fenian movement, specifically organised through the impressionable Cusack by the IRB. Its purpose was the fostering of Gaelic games and the banning of English ones (and the refusal of entry to all security forces, even the RIC) and certainly by the end of the first decade of the new century its membership was strongly IRB-influenced. The Gaelic League was established in 1893 for the purpose of restoring Irish as a literary and spoken language by a County Antrim Catholic Eoin MacNeill (1967–1945), a court clerk and self-taught scholar, and Douglas Hyde (1860–1949) the son of a Connacht clergyman who the previous year had given his inaugural address as president of the National Literary Society on the subject of 'The Necessity for De-anglicizing the Irish People'.

Both these institutions were eventually effective in their stated aims and both became highly politicised. By 1915 the patently revolutionary aims of such members of the League as Patrick Pearse and MacNeill made it impossible for Hyde to remain. For most of the first twenty years of its existence it had had a considerable number of Protestant – and even unionist – members but after 'The North Began', MacNeill's article written for the League's journal *An Claidheamh Soluis* (1899–1918) about the gun-running of the Ulster Volunteer Force (UVF) in 1912 and the resultant formation of the Irish Volunteers, it could not in any sense be regarded as non-political.

There was, then, at least an emotional awareness of a kind of historical precedent for what has since become known as the 'armed struggle' but nothing was further from the intentions of the men of 1916 than a prolonged attrition. The rationale was expressed by Pearse in one of his poems as 'bloody protest for a glorious thing' and Yeats, understanding if not approving the gesture, put it well in 'The Rose Tree', written a year after the Rising, and consisting of an imagined dialogue between Pearse and Connolly:

> There's nothing but our own red blood
> Can make a right rose tree.

All of this was clear in retrospect but few people even among the participants could have known what 'that delirium of the brave' would bring about.

2

IRISH VOLUNTEERS AND THE CITIZEN ARMY

Though speculation about 'What might have happened in history if ... ?' is the vainest of parlour games, it is possible that the perceived need for a gesture of military action, which was all the Easter Rising could hope to be, would never have arisen if the Liberal government had been able to face down the intransigence of unionist opposition to what they called with only minimal justification Rome Rule. The impasse had begun to solidify as early as 1912. In response to the Home Rule bill being presented to the Commons on 11 April of that year, 218,000 northern Protestants signed the Solemn League and Covenant. On Ulster Day (28 September) supported by Bonar Law (1858–1923) in Westminster and led at home by the Dublin lawyer Edward Carson (1854–1935) and the Belfast distiller James Craig (1871–1940) they pledged 'to use all means to prevent the present conspiracy ... '

Already thanks to the network of Orange and other lodges they had established the Ulster Volunteer Force which was to be armed with 35,000 German rifles landed

'illegally' (but with police connivance) at Larne, Bangor
and Donaghadee in April 1914, exactly a month before
the bill was finally carried. The attitude of the British
army had become clear in March in the Curragh Incident
when General Gough persuaded fifty-seven out of seventy
officers to resign their commissions rather than enforce
Home Rule in Ulster. The nature of a possible secession
was proving to be as impossible of resolution as any other
question involving the well-supported unionists who were,
as so often before, pawns in a bitter game of Westminster
politics. The Tory party had often found it advantageous
to 'play the Orange card' in the words of Lord Randolph
Churchill, the father of the Liberal government's first lord of
the admiralty, and this was to prove to be the most deadly
trick in the game. The Buckingham Palace conference of
July 1914 called by George V (reasonably assumed to be
on the side of the 'disloyalists') had solved nothing when
on 4 August Germany invaded Belgium and to everyone's
relief the matter was postponed until 'the end of hostilities'
which even the army knew would be around Christmas!

The founding of the UVF had not gone unnoticed
outside of the four unionist counties of Down, Antrim,
Armagh and Derry, nor had the successful gun-running
by the *Clydevalley*. Michael Joseph O'Rahilly (1875–1916),
a Kerry journalist who called himself 'the O'Rahilly'
and expected others to do so too, became editor of *An*

Claidheamh Soluis in 1913 and set about refurbishing it. He asked MacNeill for an editorial for the first issue of 1 November 1913 and got 'The North Began', effectively an admonition that Home Rulers should follow the union- ists' example and set up their own armed Irish Volunteers. Three weeks later on 25 November at the Rotunda rink, out of doors because of the numbers, that militia was set up with a strong involvement of the now buoyant if minus- cule IRB.

Branches were established throughout the country with, hardly surprisingly, the strongest response in Ulster. This was partly due to the organising ability of Hobson and his IRB colleague Denis McCullough (1883–1968) and partly because northern nationalists not for the first time, nor the last, felt particularly isolated and vulnerable. Redmond was slow at first to support the movement but by 14 June 1914 on being allowed to nominate half the seats on the committee had given his consent and the numbers rose to 160,000. *Their* arms running was not blinked at by the authorities. Fifteen hundred guns were landed at Howth from the *Asgard* (navigated by Erskine Childers) on 26 July 1914. The King's Own Scottish Borderers, returning to barracks, having failed to seize the guns, fired on a jeer- ing crowd in Bachelor's Walk, killing four and wounding thirty-seven. There were also many baton charges by a force of the Dublin Metropolitan Police (DMP). The incident, though caused by fatigue and misunderstood orders, shocked the nationalist population. Augustine Birrell, the genial and diplomatic chief secretary, set up a commission which found, within a fortnight, that the action of the police and army had been 'tainted with illegality' and Birrell sacked the assistant-commissioner of the DMP. The damage was done and it was believed that the official attitude to nationalists was rather different from that to Ulster Protestants.

Birrell was a clever and liberal secretary, a man of culture and a successful belletrist. His handling of affairs in Ireland was subtle and effective, maintaining close links with Redmond and Dillon, and allowing the Volunteers a lot of latitude. He did not regard them as harmless idealists, as his dispatches to the cabinet show, but he was determined not to make martyrs of them. If he was taken by surprise by the events of Easter Monday 1916 it was only because he had read MacNeill's public announcement of the cancelling of manoeuvres in the *Sunday Independent*. His perhaps inevitable resignation on 3 May, the day of the first executions, meant that affairs in Ireland were to be handled at a distance by the home secretary, which meant in practice disastrous martial law, administered by a martinet.

John Redmond had led the parliamentary party well and it had seemed that he was about to succeed where his uncrowned king had failed, but without real support from Asquith and Lloyd George he had little hope of handling the unionists. The outbreak of hostilities was a kind of relief even for him. He called for the same support for the war effort as the members of the Ulster division had shown in the north – only after they had been assured that the Home Rule bill had definitely been postponed – and he got it for a number of reasons, not all political. The original Rotunda rink members numbering at most 3,000 broke away, calling themselves the *Irish* Volunteers, as opposed to Redmond's *National* Volunteers. With MacNeill as chief of staff the leaders began to recruit supporters so that by 1916 they could count on 15,000 members. MacNeill was on the whole against a military initiative, except in the extreme case of the Volunteers' being suppressed and this was taken to be the policy of the movement as a whole. They were to be made into an effective army so that there would be no doubts about the Home Rule bill being implemented. Besides, as a practising Catholic and a pragmatist the only rising MacNeill would countenance would be one with a chance of success.

The outbreak of war, however, was regarded by the IRB as a clear example of the old Fenian dictum: England's difficulty; Ireland's opportunity. It also called to mind the prayer of the fiery Young Irelander, John Mitchel (1815–75) who had written in his *Jail Journal* (1854) 'Send war in our

time, O Lord!' Yet it was still a tiny organisation rekindled
in Ireland mainly by the old Fenian Tom Clarke, who had been
sent home in 1907 by Devoy for that purpose. His tobac-
conist shop in Great Britain Street became the centre of
IRB activity and he found a resourceful colleague in Seán
MacDermott who had joined the organisation in Belfast
through his friendship with Hobson and McCullough.
Like them he broke with Arthur Griffith's Sinn Féin
(founded with Hobson in 1905), one of the more successful alternatives to Redmond's constitutionalism, because of
its gradualism and advocacy of passive resistance.

The need for a gesture, maybe even martyrdom, was to
be formulated by Patrick Pearse, who though also a devout
Catholic felt that the justice of the IRB cause superseded
the conventional teaching of the church. This required
that for a rebellion to be legitimate a number of criteria be
met: the government must be tyrannical; the community
as a whole must approve; the tyranny be removable only
by bloodshed and its evil be greater than the effects of the
revolution; that it should have a likely chance of success.
Even the most sanguine of the IRB knew that none of
these conditions were met. The horrors of the European
war in which thousands were dying every day made the
life of young men seem cheap. The spirit of those British
who flocked to recruiting stations in August 1914, exemp-
lified in Rupert Brooke's poem 'If I Should Die ...' was

not all that far removed from Pearse's: 'The old heart of the earth needed to be warmed with the red wine of the battlefields.'

Less clear was the motivation of the two who coopted Pearse on to a military committee in 1915: Tom Clarke and Seán MacDermott, his austere lieutenant. Clarke had been a revolutionary, a member of Clan na Gael since the age of twenty-one, and had been imprisoned as a dynamitard. Perhaps he too felt that a gallant gesture, which was all any rising might be, would in time produce the effect the Fenian tradition required. The symbol of the phoenix, so dear to the movement, implied immolation. The impenetrable MacDermott who battled with poliomyelitis and suffered imprisonment under the Defence of the Realm Acts (DORA), the emergency wartime legislation, for anti-recruiting activities, continued with IRB organisation for which he had a special and fanatical talent.

The most hard-headed of the 1916 leaders was James Connolly and as trades union organiser and a Marxist intellectual the least likely to be won over by Pearse's sacrificial mysticism. Yet he too began making the same kind of noises about the need for an armed rising while the European war lasted. He was a socialist, the able lieutenant of James Larkin (1876–1947) in the Irish Transport and General Workers Union (ITGWU). He had taken over control during the infamous Dublin lock-out of 1913 and formed the Irish Citizen Army as a kind of rapid response unit to protect pickets from the often violent irruptions of the sabre-wielding DMP. Its numbers were small, not more than 350, mostly union members and, its spite of its socialist character, sufficiently nationalistic to want self-determination for Ireland. Among its more colourful members were the rebel Countess Markievicz (née Constance Gore-Booth) and the playwright Seán O'Casey who resigned when she joined. Connolly believed that though his force was small once word of an outbreak became known the whole country would rise. With the innocence of a doctrinaire Marxist he also held that a capitalist society would never destroy its own property by shelling.

When it became clear that Connolly might well initiate an independent outbreak he was invited to meet the members of the military council of the IRB. He was not seen for three days in the January of 1916 and afterwards it was obvious that he had been apprised of the council's intention to rise at Easter and that he was to be part of it. The committee now consisted of Patrick Pearse, Joseph Plunkett, Thomas MacDonagh, Thomas Clarke, Eamonn Ceannt and Seán MacDermott and part of their strategy was to deceive MacNeill. They also kept Denis McCullough, who according to the IRB constitution was president of the Irish Republic, in the dark about their intentions. MacNeill would still not countenance Volunteer involvement in any 'act of rash violence'. They would keep in readiness for their future purpose of imposing, if necessary, the limited Home Rule offered by Asquith's bill. Only the threat of its suppression or conscription in the British army would make him change his mind.

On the Wednesday of Holy Week 1916 he was given the proof he needed that suppression was imminent. A document giving details of the authorities' intention to arrest Volunteer leaders was read out at a meeting of Dublin corporation by a councillor. He immediately ordered that the Volunteers should prepare themselves for resistance but not, he insisted, for insurrection. (The complicated moves of deception were cleverly orchestrated by MacDermott and it was he who arranged that Bulmer Hobson, who had argued all along against what Pearse and his colleagues were advocating, should be kidnapped and held incommunicado for the three vital days from the evening of Good Friday until the Rising was a fact on Easter Monday.)

MacNeill was almost won over to the IRB plan especially when he was told by MacDermott that a large consignment of arms was on its way from Germany. MacDermott, convinced that MacNeill (though required for mobilisation purposes as titular head of the Volunteers) was a block to the adamant intention of the military council, tried to undermine his position by hinting that he had resigned. He had not. On Holy Saturday he learned that the castle document was a forgery prepared by MacDermott and Plunkett and that the ship with the German guns had scuttled itself in Queenstown [Cobh] harbour. He at once countermanded any orders that might have been received by Volunteers about the Easter weekend and put the advertisement in the *Sunday Independent* as confirmation.

The only effect was to postpone the Rising by a day.

3

THE PROCLAMATION

One of the most dramatic moments in what was a generally untheatrical week was one of the first: the reading on the steps of the GPO in Sackville [O'Connell] Street of the Proclamation by Pearse and its subsequent pasting to the wall. The 500-word document is a fine piece of rhetoric and in its restraint and lack of quasi-religious emotionalism (except in the apostrophe to the Most High God in the final paragraph) not entirely the work of Pearse himself. It claimed the Rising as an IRB gesture, a means of recovering the phoenix flame after the farce of '67 but it also associated with the IRB the Volunteers and the Citizen Army. This was a large claim since relatively few members of these bodies were involved. The Rising was not so much a minority happening as one involving a minority of three minorities.

It was sociologically ahead of its time in its suggestion of a welfare state and feminist in its stated equality of the sexes, a clear indication of input by Connolly. Its tone was remarkably in contrast to the attitudes of the Volunteers as a whole, whose rhetoric emphasised 'manly' deeds and tended to patronise the members of Cumann na mBan (its auxiliary corps set up in 1914) as earlier Sinn Féin had seemed condescending, in the language of the *Zeitgeist*, towards its older sororial organisation Inghinidhe na hÉireann (set up by Maud Gonne in 1900). It recognised that the women involved (over ninety with sixty from Cumann na mBan) were sharing the risks of the men and though they on the whole took no part in the actual fighting they were used for the much more dangerous job of dispatch-carrying, as well as serving as field nurses and cooks.

The seven signatories were taking upon themselves the ultimate responsibility and all had a pretty clear idea of what the outcome would be for them at any rate. Because of the myth-making, not to say hagiography, that tended to characterise accounts of the Rising, at least for the first fifty years, it is difficult for those who grew up with the myth to realise that the signatories and the other men made famous by their deaths were relatively unknown even in the notoriously village-city that was the Dublin of the time. Yeats may have met them with vivid faces but they were coming from counter or desk.

Pearse (b. 1879) had become a barrister but his only recorded case, which he lost, was in the defence of a Done-gal man who had contravened the regulations by having

his name in Irish on his cart. He was chiefly known as
a writer, Gaelic activist and education theorist who had
found his own school, St Enda's in Ranelagh, later moving
to Rathfarnham. Ceannt (b. 1881) was a corporation clerk
and chiefly famous for having played the uileann pipes for
Pius X at his golden jubilee in 1908. MacDermott (b. 1881)
– who signed himself Seán Mac Diarmada – had been a
tram conductor and was the longest serving member of
the IRB apart from Clarke (b. 1857). Plunkett (b. 1887),
the youngest of the signatories, was the son of a hereditary
papal count and found it necessary to travel for health
reason but had been a prominent figure in Dublin literary
circles. The best known were MacDonagh (b. 1878) and
Connolly (b. 1868) but for strikingly different reasons.
MacDonagh was a poet, playwright and academic critic
and a lecturer in English in UCD; Connolly had been
an effective and unpopular ITGWU official in Belfast
and either loved or hated as Larkin's deputy. Of the others
who died Willie Pearse (b. 1881), brother of Patrick, was
a sculptor and art teacher in St Enda's; Edward Daly (b.
1891), brother-in-law of Tom Clarke, had worked in a
bakery and wholesale chemist; Michael O'Hanrahan (b.
1877) was a journalist and Michael Mallin (b. 1880) a silk
weaver; Con Colbert (b. 1888) also worked in a bakery;
Seán Heuston (b. 1891) had been a railway worker; John
MacBride (b. 1865), famous as the estranged husband of

Maud Gonne, had fought for the Boers and was employed by Dublin Waterworks; Tom Kent (b. c. 1867) who was shot in Cork military detention barracks after surrender in a gun battle had been a farmer. Eamon de Valera (b. 1882) the only leader to escape the firing-squad, because of Redmond's intervention with Asquith, had been a lecturer in mathematics. The rebellion was neither plebeian nor bourgeois but drew its participants from a vertical section through the Irish society of the time.

Pearse was the main rhetorician who found the words to express the particular sacrifice that the small band of patriots were about to make. A poem entitled 'Christmas 1915' reads:

> O King that was born
> To set bondsmen free,
> In the coming battle,
> Help the Gael.

And his funeral oration at the grave of the old Fenian, O'Donovan Rossa, in Glasnevin on 1 August 1915, though scarcely heard because of the crowds, the presence of a larger armed force of Redmond's National Volunteers (there because O'Donovan Rossa for the last years of his life was if anything a Redmondite) and his own poor delivery, became a sacred text. It reiterated his conviction: 'Life springs from death; and from the graves of patriot men and women spring living nations' and its conclusion was the inflammatory: 'The fools, the fools, the fools! – they have left us our Fenian dead, and while Ireland holds these graves, Ireland unfree shall never be at peace!'

One of the mantras that has come down from the time is 'Sixteen Dead Men', the title of another poem about the Rising by Yeats who by the time of writing was happy to be accounted if not true brother of this company too, then at least a close relation. The sixteenth was not shot but hanged as a traitor in Pentonville Prison, London on 3 August and the phrase from the Proclamation, 'gallant allies in Europe' was a vain tribute to the work he had tried to do. This was Roger Casement (b. 1864), who was brought up in County Antrim and having joined the British consular service in 1895 was knighted for humanitarian services because of reports of mistreatment of native workers in the Congo and South America. He was always of strong nationalist sympathies and having joined the Volunteers argued that the only hope of a successful rising lay with German guns and an Irish brigade of prisoners-of-war.

He made his way to Berlin from New York in 1914 and travelled to Limburg, near Koblenz where the German authorities, only too anxious to cooperate with an enemy of England and no doubt thinking, 'England's difficulty is Germany's opportunity', had collected 2,000 Irish prisoners. He was unsuccessful in establishing the Irish brigade and generally got a poor reception. He was not an ideal recruiting officer, his neuroticism imperfectly concealed. The Germans were naturally disappointed since their support for a possible rising was anti-British rather than pro-Irish. Casement remained in Germany, 'a virtual prisoner' and unwell most of the time.

Plunkett was sent in April 1915 by the usual circuitous route through neutral countries to tell Casement about the IRB's plans and to ask for 50,000 rifles and ammunition. Casement advised him that no rising should take place, especially when their German contacts refused their request and advised them that they should look to America where there were millions of Irishmen with money to supply their needs. There was to be no Irish brigade and the IRB military council should be so informed; it is believed that Plunkett did not deliver the message but in view of the mind-set of the inner council it would have been ignored any way. In February 1916 Devoy through the German ambassador in Washington asked the German High Command for 100,000 rifles, for artillery and German officers. All the Germans offered were 20,000 rifles (captured from Russia on the eastern front), ten machine guns and five million rounds. These would be landed in Kerry and distributed to the Volunteers in Munster and Connacht in preparation for a simultaneous revolt. Casement knew this shipment to be totally inadequate and made his way to Ireland to insist that the Rising be called off. He travelled on the *U–19*, the submarine escort of the arms ship the *Libau*, which was masquerading as a Norwegian trawler the *Aud*.

The *Aud* eluded the British blockade and appeared in Tralee Bay on Holy Thursday, four days earlier than the arranged rendezvous. She waited twenty-four hours for some signal and then, intercepted by the royal navy, was being escorted into Queenstown when the captain, Karl Spindler scuttled the ship with the German flag flying. That same day, Good Friday, Casement nearly drowned as his dinghy capsized on Banna Strand and later, exhausted and dispirited, he was arrested and taken to Tralee. There would be neither arms nor men from the gallant allies in Europe but nothing was going to stop the IRB's bloody sacrifice.

4

EASTER WEEK

The number who turned out was about 1,500, consisting of Volunteers, Citizen Army, Cumann na mBan, and Fianna Éireann (the National boy scouts). The majority (including Pearse, Connolly, Clarke, MacDermott and Plunkett) occupied the General Post Office in Sackville [O'Connell] Street as headquarters. (Their taking over was not without a certain comedy in that at least one customer insisted on completing his purchase of stamps before leaving.) A group known as the First Battalion Irish Volunteers, led by Commandant Edward Daly, occupied the Four Courts and set up posts at Jameson's distillery and various buildings in the Church Street–North King Street area. The Mendicity Institute across the Liffey on Usher's Island, was taken over by D Company under the command of Captain Seán Heuston. MacDonagh, in charge of the Second Battalion, took over Jacob's biscuit factory in Bishop Street near St Stephen's Green, which had been occupied by Mallin of the Citizen Army with Countess Markievicz as second in command. Boland's bakery and flour mill were taken by de Valera and he set up outposts on the railway between

Westland Row and Lansdowne Road at Mount Street Bridge on the Grand Canal. Ceannt with Cathal Brugha took over the South Dublin Union with deployments at Marrowbone Lane, Ardee Street and Cork Street. Seán Connolly, one of the first casualties, and a company of Citizen Army members occupied the City Hall.

The emplacements formed a rough ring around the GPO headquarters and were placed near some of the British barracks. In fact Beggar's Bush barracks was effectively unmanned, as was Dublin Castle. Trinity College with its thick sixteenth-century walls was virtually empty of students or soldiers. The original strategy was devised by Plunkett, now very ill, and Connolly, and seemed to consist of holding out until spontaneous risings west of the Shannon would seize most of Munster and Connacht and personnel then march on the capital. Without the promised arms from Germany and given the welter of command and counter-command this could not happen. Clarke, however, believed that they could withstand counter-attack for months, by which time the war would surely be over and the IRB have its place at a post-war conference table. The failure of nerve of the rebels at the Castle was an indication of military inexperience and it was characteristic that Seán Connolly was shot raising a flag on buildings opposite. Another example of military incompetence was the failure to cut all communications.

Though the total number of troops in the city was about 1,200, reinforcements were soon on their way from Belfast, the Curragh, Templemore and Athlone, summoned by telephone.

The first incident occurred in Phoenix Park when a body of Volunteers, having set out even before the reading of the Proclamation, failed to blow up the arms dump at the Magazine Fort. The first casualty was the seventeen-year-old son of the fort's commander who was shot as he tried to reach a telephone to raise the alarm. The unarmed DMP sergeant on duty at the outer gate of the Castle was another early casualty but the full bitterness of what any violent rising may mean was not understood until four o'clock when a band of the Irish Volunteer Defence Corps, a middle-aged group of Irishmen forming a reserve group of the British army, were attacked as they were returning to Beggar's Bush after a route march. These, known locally as the Gorgeous Wrecks from the 'GR' they wore on their armbands and carrying unloaded rifles, were raked with bullets. Five died and nine were wounded.

The first tactical manoeuvre (in an adventure that saw few) was made by Mallin and Markievicz when they realised that St Stephen's Green was vulnerable to fire from the Shelbourne Hotel on the north side and that their digging of trenches had been a waste of effort. They took over the Royal College of Surgeons on the west side but were driven out by reinforced British fire the next afternoon. The only serious activity from the GPO headquarters was the shooting of four Lancers in Sackville [O'Connell] Street on that Monday afternoon. The first soldiers to engage the rebels were from the Dublin Fusiliers and the Royal Irish Rifles but already a mob of Dubliners, alert to the fact that the police had been withdrawn, had begun looting from the fashionable shops in Sackville Street. Someone said that the reading of the Proclamation at 12.45 by Pearse, not a great speaker at the best of times, was drowned out by the sound of breaking glass.

By the coming of night in what had been a fine sunny spring day the crowds from Fairyhouse races and other Bank Holiday treats returned to a terribly changed Dublin. The death roll included civilians as well as Volunteers, police and soldiers. The moods of amusement, bemusement and perplexity had hardened to rage and hatred. The Irish, then as now, had sufficient political awareness to understand that what had been agreed national policy and implied the deaths of many of the countrymen in Flanders was being challenged and perhaps eroded. One eye-witness of the time, recorded in *Curious Journey*, the oral history compiled by Kenneth Griffith and Timothy O'Grady, describes how when he arrived at Jacob's on the Tuesday morning, 'the place was surrounded by a howling mob roaring at the Volunteers inside, "Come out to France and fight you lot of so-and-so slackers.'"

Over the Post Office flew two strange flags, one green with the words Irish Republic painted in gold, and a tri-colour of green, white and orange, another gesture of wish-ful thinking in its implicit idea of reconciliation, a relic of Young Ireland. Above the roof of the Imperial Hotel flew the Citizen Army flag: a plough with a sword on its coulter and decked with seven stars. It socialist credentials were impeccable but it was to give a title to a play which in its emotional truth about Easter Week was to prove un-palatable to the post-revolutionary audiences.

By Tuesday General Lowe had declared martial law in Dublin city and county, having now 5,000 troops at his disposal. His strategy was to keep an unbreachable line of troops along an east-west axis that would separate the posts on the north side of the Liffey, including the GPO headquarters, from the rest. He soon recovered control of a line between Kingsbridge Station and Trinity. He also had four pieces of artillery which came from Athlone and were set up near Prussia Street and in Phibsborough above the Cabra Road. It was typical of the informal nature of the affair that a private in the Dublin Fusiliers could stop a Volunteer friend in Dorset Street to warn him that the guns were on the way and to get the message to the GPO. The shelling began and continued for the rest of the week, gradually destroying the buildings in the centre of the city and showing no regard for capitalist principles. It did increase the anger of the populace and made looting somewhat more hazardous.

That day the Citizen Army battalion came under such fire from the Shelbourne and the United Services Club that they were forced to abandon their position in the College of Surgeons. A four-page newspaper called the *Irish War News* was printed in Liberty Hall and had optimistic news that 'The Republican forces hold the lines taken up at twelve noon on Easter Monday, and nowhere, despite fierce and almost continuous attacks of the British forces, have the lines been broken through.' It also urged civilians to build barricades in the streets to oppose the advance of the British troops – in other words to invite death while totally unarmed. The equality principles of the Proclamation had slipped somewhat:

> There is work for everyone; for the men in the fighting line, and for the women in the provision of food and first aid.

The main roles for the women volunteers were as the *War News* described them. There were sixty from Cumann na mBan and they catered and cared for the men in the various posts. Their services were not always appreciated nor were they all equally skilled. *Curious Journey* recalls an occasion in the Four Courts kitchen when they made tea by putting a pound of the dry leaves into the water left over from boiling turnips. The result was indescribable and Seán Howard, the man who took the first mouthful, cried, 'Well you're Cumann na mBan maybe, but it's Cumann na Monsters you are. You want to kill us off.' (The book also records that Howard was shot the next day while carrying a dispatch to Piaras Beaslaí in the Father Matthew Hall in Church Street.) One commander refused to allow any women into his post. This was de Valera and long afterwards he offended one of the women of 1916, the feminist and suffragist Hanna Sheehy-Skeffington, by confiding that it was probably a mistake since he had to release some of his men for the 'womanly' tasks of nursing and making meals.

By now, although there were no newspapers, the word was getting out that something unusual was happening in Dublin. Some Volunteers tried to get to Dublin, in spite of MacNeill's prohibition, but found it impossible to get near the rebel posts. The Volunteers were strong in Tyrone and when the word came of events in Dublin they turned out in Carrickmore in pouring rain; Donaghmore and Coalisland waited for orders and did not mobilise until the Tuesday morning at 11 o'clock but went home again, their leader Dr Patrick McCartan (1878–1963) having to hide out in a barn in the Sperrins. There was a similar inconclusive mustering of 132 men in the Falls Road by Denis McCullough but their plan to join with the Tyrone

Volunteers and make their way to Galway collapsed when the Tyrone men refused to move.

On the Monday afternoon the County Louth contingent under Seán MacEntee (afterwards a leading Fianna Fáil politician) had killed a policeman and a guards officer from among their prisoners. There was a low-level and soon abandoned operation against a police station in Galway while the Volunteers in Limerick on stand-by on Easter Sunday stood down on receiving MacNeill's countermand and, knowing of the loss of the *Aud*, ignored Pearse's final order. In Enniscorthy the local battalion took over the town on Tuesday morning and surrendered to the military on Vinegar Hill on the Friday. Cork mustered 1,000 men on Easter Sunday, but they went home having received nine different sets of instructions, each new one contradicting the last.

One other event of the Tuesday has lived in infamy: a captain of the Royal Irish Rifles called Bowen-Colthurst arrested two journalists, Patrick McIntyre and Thomas Dickson and the well-known pacifist Francis Sheehy-Skeffington. None had had anything to do with the Rising, though Sheehy-Skeffington was trying to organise a citizens' band to prevent looting and his wife Hanna was a messenger in the GPO. The next morning on his own initiative Bowen-Colthurst had them shot, the bungled operation requiring two firing-squads. It was known that on the Tuesday evening while out on patrol and having Sheehy-Skeffington with him as a hostage he had deliberately shot a boy called Coade in Rathmines. A court-martial insisted upon by a senior officer, Sir Francis Vane, in spite of Castle inertia found Bowen-Colthurst of unsound mind, but Hanna Sheehy-Skeffington continued demands for further action until a royal commission made an apology and an offer of monetary compensation which she refused.

Wednesday saw the first Republican surrender when Heuston had to evacuate the Mendicity Institute which was nearest to Lowe's central chain of firepower. MacDonagh's men in Jacob's were holding out with few casualties but Ceannt in the South Dublin Union was under continuous fierce attack. The British heavy firepower was greatly improved by the fitting out of a boat, the *Helga*, as an artillery platform. She anchored in the Liffey near the North Wall and soon demolished Liberty Hall and removed the top storey of the GPO. She continued to pound the city centre until Sackville [O'Connell] Street was reduced to rubble and the gold lettering on the flag above the beleaguered Post Office had turned dark brown.

Yet it was on the same day that the Volunteers had their most impressive military success and learned many lessons for the future. Reinforcements had arrived at Kingstown in the shape of two companies of the Sherwood Foresters.

They were welcomed by the majority of Dubliners as saviours but consisted of new recruits, most of whom had been in the army for less than three months. They came from Nottingham as part of the deadly 'comrades' recruiting initiative which meant that whole streets, factory workshops, village populations all joined up together and died together. The gossip about the city was that some of them thought they had landed in France. One column made their way safely along the Stillorgan Road to the Royal Hospital. As the other marched along Northumberland Road towards Mount Street Bridge to cross the Grand Canal they were caught in crossfire from de Valera's outposts. It took many hours for them to force their way across the canal and at the cost of four officers killed and fourteen wounded and 216 ORs killed or seriously injured. The total number of Volunteers in the engagement was put as two in a house in Haddington Road, three in Northumberland Road and seven in Clanwilliam House on Mount Street. The fire was so persistent and so rapid that the rifles of the insurgents were cooled with oil from sardine tins, probably their main rations. One of the men in 25 Northumberland Road, Lieutenant Michael Malone, was killed and of the seven who held Clanwilliam House from noon till 8 p.m. three died. The rest, covered by sniper fire, retreated to Boland's only after the house had been set on fire.

On Thursday it was realised that all lines of communication between headquarters and the other positions were finally cut. Connolly on reconnaissance in the streets around the Post Office, now hardly defendable, was shot twice in the leg and in the various Volunteer emplacements the talk was of evacuation, if not actual surrender. Brugha was seriously wounded in an attack on the South Dublin Union but by sheer ferocity he and the other defenders beat the British back.

Birrell returned on the Friday accompanying General Sir John Maxwell, who was to take over as commander in chief. Maxwell was to say rashly to Lord Wimbourne, the lord lieutenant, 'I am going to ensure that there will be no treason whispered for a hundred years.' His first announcement on arrival was: 'If necessary I shall not hesitate to destroy all buildings within any area occupied by the rebels.' This was indicative of the wisdom and delicacy with which he would handle the aftermath of surrender. He and Lowe had now 20,000 British troops deployed and the city centre was cordoned off. It was a day of attrition with shellfire growing more and more accurate, streets raked with machine-gun bullets, and charging and dismantling of barricades the main military activity.

Pearse had issued another communiqué at 9.30 a.m. reassuring those who had fought that they had 'redeemed Dublin from many shames, and made her name splendid among the names of cities.' He then dismissed the women and girls, shaking hands with each as they left. By evening the GPO was on fire and the Cumann na mBan members who were still on duty and the wounded were moved back to Jervis Street Hospital. The remaining Volunteers decided to make a dash through Moore Street to Great Britain Street but they did not know that Henry Street was continuously under British fire mainly from the Rotunda. The O'Rahilly volunteered to reconnoitre Henry Street to see if it was worth trying to reach Moore Street. Before he left he made sure that thirteen prisoners who had been held in the GPO were safe before heading out. He was shot in Moore Lane. (He was one of the men whom Yeats remembered with typical affection. He had delivered Mac-Neill's orders to Kerry and Limerick but headed for Dublin himself, and in the ballad 'The O'Rahilly' Yeats has him say to Pearse and Connolly:

> Because I helped to wind the clock
> I come to hear it strike.

Most of the rest of the men in the Post Office got out in spite of the slaughtering fire, MacDermott and Plunkett managing to get a van pulled across Henry Street. Three women who had stayed got safely across to Moore Street, as did Pearse, though in his dash he stumbled and the others thought he had been hit. Connolly, now on a stretcher, was also carried to safety. There were seventeen casualties during the operation and when the others settled into 16 Moore Street they were able to break through the walls of houses to give them a frontage on Great Britain Street. It was clear to even the most sanguine that the fighting was about over.

There was to be one other operation on that Friday which has become part of the mythology. Thomas Ashe, with Richard Mulcahy (who took command of the Free State forces after the death of Michael Collins in August 1922) as lieutenant, engaged a force of the paramilitary RIC at Ashbourne on the road to Slane about thirteen miles from Dublin. Ashe was from County Kerry and was principal of Lusk national school. He became commander of the County Meath Volunteers and his ambush was an anticipation of the tactics that were to be employed during the Anglo-Irish War that would start three years later. A party of forty RIC men led by a chief inspector were on their way to relieve the barracks at Ashbourne and they were effectively ambushed at a crossroads about a mile north of the town. The fight lasted for five hours and when the police ran out of ammunition they surrendered. Eight had been killed and fifteen wounded. Ashe's company had up till then moved freely about the county attacking barracks and doing what they could to disrupt communications.

The Battle of Ashbourne and the Battle of Mount Street were really the only effective encounters of the week. They would be studied by the next set of insurgents, especially by Michael Collins, who took command of what was now called Sinn Féin on the death of Ashe from pneumonia brought on by force feeding during his hunger strike in Mountjoy in 1917.

The Rising was effectively finished and by the Saturday morning the decision to seek terms from Lowe had been made. It is said that it was the shooting of a publican and his family while running out of one of the houses carrying a white flag that persuaded Pearse that it was time to call a halt. Connolly, who with the exception of MacBride was the only one with military experience and who had supervised whatever minimal tactics were devised in the Post Office, agreed. He had said on the Monday, 'We are going out to be slaughtered', and probably felt that too many others were being needlessly slaughtered as well.

A Cumann na mBan nurse, Elizabeth O'Farrell, carried a white flag and this message to the British barricade at Great Britain Street:

> The Commandant-General of the Irish Republican Army wishes to treat with the Commandant-General of the British forces in Ireland.

Lowe demanded an unconditional surrender and at 3.30 p.m. Pearse, wearing a great coat and a Boer War slouch hat handed his sword to Lowe. At 3.45 he signed the typed order of stand-down:

In order to prevent the further slaughter of Dublin citizens, and in the hope of saving the lives of our followers now surrounded and hopelessly outnumbered, the members of the Provisional Government present at Headquarters have agreed to unconditional surrender, and the Commandants of the various districts in the City and County will order their commands to lay down their arms.

The order had to be counter-signed by Connolly since the Citizen Army recognised no leader but him:

I agree to these conditions for the men only under my command in the Moore Street district and for the men in the Stephen's Green command.

At nine o'clock that evening the Volunteers, apart from those in Jacob's and Boland's and the South Dublin Union, marched from Moore Street along Sackville [O'Connell] Street and dumped their arms at the foot of the five-year-old Parnell statue. Then they were made to lie on the grass in the Rotunda grounds. Later that evening a British officer called Lee Wilson amused himself by stripping Clarke naked and parading him in view of the nurses who were looking out the windows of the hospital. Clarke, in his sixtieth year, was by the standards of the time an elderly man and it was a particularly cruel thing to do to a person of known prudery. Watching the humiliation was Michael Collins, who was able to announce five years later: 'We got him [Lee Wilson] today in Gorey.'

MacDonagh, with most of his force intact, refused to

accept the order until he had spoken to Pearse, a prisoner in Richmond Barracks, and then had difficulty in persuading Ceannt to surrender. His addition to Pearse's order read:

> On consultation with Commandant Ceannt and other officers I have decided to agree to unconditional surrender also.

The greatest difficulty was experienced by de Valera at the garrison at Boland's mills. The defences had not been breached – unlike most of the other emplacements it was a tactical building – and the men were prepared for a much longer siege. When they did obey the order, many broke their rifles in dismay on the ground.

The most notable thing about the city that day was the ending of the noise of the fighting as Brighid Lyons Thornton, who was one of the Cumann na mBan members in the Four Courts, described it in *Curious Journey*:

> And then Saturday morning, louder than all the noise was the silence that descended upon the city.

She also recalled that after the surrender:

> ... some of the Church Street priests came in and lambasted us with abuse all night for doing what we did. They disapproved highly of the rebellion, of the damage to the city and the people who were killed and whose homes were burned.

The church could not approve the Rising since it met none of the moral criteria, and the Dublin priests shared the feelings of dismay and anger of the majority population. A number of Capuchin fathers, Augustine, Columbus, Aloysius, Sebastian and Albert, were allowed to minister to those condemned to death, and Aloysius and Augustine travelled from post to post in Lowe's car, which he had put at their disposal, as *bona fides* that Pearse had signed the surrender. Yet one initially reluctant curate from the pro-cathedral, Fr John Flanagan, became a kind of unofficial chaplain in the Post Office, hearing confessions, giving extreme unction to the dying and helping the Volunteers move to the Moore Street post on the Friday, giving them absolution before the reckless evacuation. He also cheered the men up by eating chicken with them on the Friday.

As such things go the casualties were light: of the Volunteers sixty-four were dead excluding those who would later be executed; 134 soldiers killed or dead of wounds while 318 were wounded; seventeen policemen from the DMP and the RIC, the latter mainly at Ashbourne, and five 'Gorgeous Wrecks'. It was the civilians who suffered most with at least 220 killed and wounded in excess of 600. The centre of the city was rubble and indeed in the rough ellipse formed by the Circular Roads many buildings were damaged. The fury of the populace was vented early; Brighid Lyons Thornton describes how the women, led by the rebel countess, needed the protection of the army as they were marched towards Kilmainham from the Four Courts.

Never did I see such savage women. A lot of them were getting the separation allowance because their husbands were off fighting in France and they thought their livelihood would be taken away because of what we did.

The role of Cumann na mBan members was generally caring for the wounded and preparing food for the men but not all the women were content to be help-mates. Fifteen of them, members of the Citizen Army, fought beside the men in St Stephen's Green and the College of Surgeons. These included Countess Markievicz who had trained Na Fianna, the boys brigade, who were drilled and taught the use of arms (most of them were sent home 'with a kick in the pants' and not interned; Seán Lemass, later the great moderniser of Ireland, was one shown that rough mercy) and as commander of a battalion of troops she engaged in hostile fire. Margaret Skinnider (c. 1893–1971), the Glasgow feminist, was bravest (or rashest), tried to blow up the Shelbourne and was a daring rooftop sniper. She held logically that the political and social equality that she was struggling for required equality of risk. A crack shot, she was wounded in an attack on a machine-gun post and arrested from St Vincent's Hospital. Kathleen Lynn (1874–1955), the daughter of an Anglican canon and one of the first women to graduate in medicine from the Royal University, was the Citizen Army chief medical officer and negotiated the surrender of the City Hall emplacement.

Madeleine ffrench-Mullen (1890–1944) who ran the medical post in St Stephen's Green, was to join with Dr Lynn in founding St Ultan's Infant Hospital in Charlemont Street in 1919. A sixteen-year-old Molly O'Reilly (c. 1900–1950) was the City Hall dispatch carrier.

In light of this level of participation it was perfectly appropriate that it should have been a woman who parlayed with the officer in charge at the barricade in Great Britain Street. Seventy women in all were arrested and Markievicz was condemned to death but reprieved. Her colleague Helen Molony, the trade-union organiser and Abbey actress who had taken part in the attack on Dublin Castle, was also interned. One heroine of the Rising was not in Dublin but played her part in Kerry, making arrangements for the reception of the *Aud*. This was Kathleen Timoney (c. 1889–1972) whose baby, christened Pearse, of course, was born on 3 May 1916!

Birrell in one of his last dispatches had advised Asquith and the Liberal cabinet that the Rising was not an *Irish* rebellion: 'It would be a pity if *post facto* it became one'. Birrell's advice was usually sound and just as usually ignored. He resigned as chief secretary on 3 May when with deaths of Pearse, Clarke and MacDonagh Maxwell had taken the first steps to make it very much an *Irish* rebellion – if not *the* Irish rebellion.

5

THE EXECUTIONS

It is hard to determine exactly when the mood of betrayal and rage began to change. The surrender was followed by wholesale arrests of many who had had no connection with the Rising. 3,430 men and seventy-nine women were arrested but of these 1,424 men and all but five of the women were released within six weeks. These five included Kathleen Clarke, soon to be the widow of Tom Clarke and designated to lead the IRB should the members of the military council be killed. One-hundred-and-seventy men and Countess Markievicz were imprisoned while 1,836 men and five women were interned, mainly at Frongoch in present-day Gwyned.

Asquith had agreed that the 'ringleaders' be dealt with in the 'most severe way possible' and Redmond had acquiesced. John Dillon disagreed with his leader and kept haranguing Maxwell about the short-sightedness of his policy. In fact ninety death sentences were passed and seventy-five of them commuted. What made the disposal of 'the ringleaders' so appalling and politically unwise was the piecemeal nature of the executions. On Wednesday 3 May, a mere four days after the surrender, the official announcement was made:

> Three signatories of the notice proclaiming the Irish Republic, P. H. Pearse, T. MacDonagh, and T. J. Clarke have been tried by Field Court Martial and sentenced to death. The sentence having been duly confirmed the three above-mentioned men were shot this morning.

The first of the martyrs were shot at dawn in the yard of Kilmainham; the usual humane decencies were not observed in that while they received holy communion the priest was not allowed to be with them at the end in spite of his promise. A tiny crack appeared in the granite façade of Maxwell's harshness in that Mrs Pearse was allowed to visit her second son William and the widow of Thomas Clarke her brother, Edward Daly, both due to be shot the next day along with Michael O'Hanrahan and the terminally-ill Joseph Plunkett. He was married to the artist Grace Gifford by candlelight, because of a power failure, in the prison chapel at midnight a few hours before the dawn execution. The prison chaplain Fr Eugene McCarthy officiated. None of the bodies were allowed burial in consecrated ground but were burned with quicklime, the common means of disposal of convicted murderers. The others might conceivably have been regarded as 'ringleaders' but Willie Pearse was shot simply because he was Patrick's brother.

The simultaneous announcement that seventeen other court-martial sentences had been commuted to penal service did nothing to mitigate the perceived cruelty of the military reaction. If anything it seemed part of a cold game of cat-and-mouse. Redmond, already regretting his stance, kept appealing for clemency in the Commons and visited Asquith daily. Asquith wired Maxwell that there should be no more executions but he was ignored and Redmond did not, as he had threatened, resign. The Liberal party was showing its usual inability to challenge the war office and the senior military establishment. John MacBride was shot on 5 May in spite of his total ignorance of the IRB's intentions before Easter Monday (he wasn't trustworthy enough). He had, however, told the court that he had stared down the barrels of British rifles far too often in the past to be afraid of death. And though he was in Yeats' eyes 'a drunken vainglorious lout' he too was numbered in the song. The flamboyant reputation of his estranged wife who had figured in Castle records for more than a decade may have played its part in his selection for death.

The executions (and the commutations) continued in spite of near-frantic appeals by members of the Irish party. Maxwell who with military logic regarded the Rising as a German plot to discommode Britain on the eve of the great putsch on the Somme was coming under pressure from southern unionists to be even more draconian. Col-

bert, Ceannt, Mallin and Heuston were shot on 8 May
and Connolly and MacDermott on the twelfth. The
deliberateness of the executions and the stringing out of
them over ten days was described later by the Countess of
Fingall as a 'stream of blood coming from beneath a closed
door'. Maxwell conceded to Asquith that Connolly's and
MacDermott's would be the last, although no one outside
government circles knew this. They could not be sure
that the blood had stopped. Asquith had announced in
the Commons on 10 May that thirteen executions had
taken place, seventy-three people had been sentenced to
penal servitude and six to hard labour while 1,706 were
deported.

The prisoners were treated badly, especially as they were
being transported to English jails in Stafford, Wakefield,
Lewes, Knutsford, Glasgow, Perth. Later they were transferred to the Frongoch internment camp. Their spirits
were generally high and 'A Soldier's Song' was bawled out
at every excuse. They were gratified too that as they were
marched to their less than palatial transports (often cattle
boats) they were cheered by the people. The women who
had pelted them with eggs and tomatoes in April now came
forward to kiss them and fill their pockets with gifts.

It was not only at home that opinion was changing.
The *Manchester Guardian*, the leading liberal paper of
the day, declared that the executions 'were becoming an

atrocity'. The British ambassador in Washington, who had reassured the cabinet that public opinion was against the Rising, had a different story to tell after news of the executions became known. The fact that many of those who had taken part were poets as an instant anthology *Poems of the Irish Revolutionary Brotherhood* (1916), published in Boston, clearly showed, undermined any attempt to write them off as heartless gunmen. Publication of substantial work by Pearse, Plunkett and MacDonagh soon after their deaths had the effect on the British reading public of having to take what they said seriously. World opinion was turning against the British and too late they did what they could to limit the damage. Just before Christmas 600 internees who were untried were welcomed home with countrywide jubilation (except in the predictable areas of the north) and by 16 June 1917 all the prisoners were released, including de Valera, MacNeill (whose arrest and that of Griffith provided clear evidence of the wrongheadedness of Maxwell's policy) and Markievicz.

It was clear that the country's freedom from treason would not last the hundred years prophesied by Maxwell and it was largely his own fault. Other reasons for the country's change of heart were a general increase of anglophobia and the growing conviction that the Liberals were not to be trusted. The dignity of the Volunteers who had taken part in the Rising and their undoubted heroism also

played their part. The mass of the Irish population felt that
they had been honoured rather than disgraced and when
the story of Sheehy-Skeffington and the apparent early
unconcern of the military authorities became known there
was general affront.

And so in spite of all efforts the Rising achieved its
purpose; the country was united and militant and through
no fault of its worthy leader Redmondism was dead. The
full extent of the support for Sinn Féin was evident in
the immediately postwar general election when the party
won seventy-three of the country's 105 seats to the Home
Rule party's six. The time of imprisonment had been for
the Volunteers (and those who had been arrested without
cause) a crash course in Irish culture, nationality and
revolution. And under new and more ruthless leaders that
revolution came. Elizabeth Bowen summed up the feeling
of the time in her history of the Shelbourne (1951):

> Executions, wholesale arrests, deportations savoured to Ire-
> land of Cromwellian reprisals; they were to combine to
> plough 1916 deep in among the other race-memories in the
> country's heart. There was to be much more of it to come.

Yet the Irish are a resilient people and she could not help
adding:

> As for the Shelbourne, it woke from a bad dream. Sandbags
> gone, soldiers out, staff back, it returned to normal in (virtu-
> ally) the twinkling of an eye.

6

AFTERMATH

The events of Easter Week have been the subject of much writing, both hagiographic and revisionist. The Proclamation, the communiqués, the statement of surrender, Pearse's poems, especially those written before his execution, became a series of near-sacred texts. The accounts of Plunkett's marriage and the ten minutes that the couple were allowed together, MacDonagh's dying 'like a prince', as the presiding officers recalled, Connolly's execution strapped to a chair because of his gangrenous leg, the commutation of de Valera's death sentence (wrongly believed to have resulted from American diplomatic intervention, though Redmond and Dillon who secured it from Asquith may have emphasised in the negotiations that he had been born of a Spanish father and an Irish mother in Manhattan), all combined to make a heady mythology that became the staple learning of the children of the Free State.

The nature of the Rising and the British response made the Anglo-Irish War inevitable and its greater brutality was realised to be of the nature of such warfare. The Civil War which followed and which was if anything more grisly also had its roots in 1916. It set in motion the process which would result in Saorstát Éireann and in time give most of the Irish people an approximation of what Pearse, Collins and Griffith had fought for. But it also gave respectability to the partitioning of the country which though unwanted even by the unionists was given to them on the best possible terms. The losers, the ones on whom the Rising inflicted the most grievous injury, were the nationalists of the six counties, chosen with precision to make part of the province governable as a one-party state with Catholics the victims of severe and institutionalised apartheid. It is one of the ironies of the years that followed partition that nowhere were the icons of 1916 more devoutly worshipped than in Tyrone and Derry City and in West Belfast.

The men and women of 1916 were on the whole admirable, idealistic and civilised, and their policies, in so far as their implications were understood, liberal and non-sectarian. Their self-sacrifice was understood by them at least to be no more that a glorious statement of belief. They did what they could to keep their fight honourable and temporary. Yet the subsequent coarsening of their ideals in the minds of some who came later did them less than justice. The seventy-fifth anniversary of the Rising in 1991 was a notably less vocal and less confident affair than the fiftieth. A majority of people could not help contrast

the five or six days of glory with thirty years of murderous attrition in Northern Ireland, and, what would have
hurt Pearse and MacDonagh more, effectively sectarian
conflict, for all the double-think of the apologists for the
continuance of the 'armed struggle'. The colder eye turned
upon the events and personalities of Easter Week not just
by historians but by most Irish people was rooted in the
argument: if the violence and terror and cruelty are the
logical outcome of the Volunteer ideals then perhaps they
were always fundamentally flawed.

Another dubious legacy, some argue, is the embracing
and advocacy of the ultimate sacrifice ar *son na hÉireann*.
This was expressed succinctly by Sir Arnold Bax (1883–
1953), in a banned poem 'A Dublin Ballad – 1916':

> To all true Irishmen on earth
> Arrest and death come late or soon.

The actions of the Rising were taken and its principles
formulated when by late-twentieth-century standards the
lives of young men were cheap. By the time a second
apocalyptic war had finished, the more pragmatic felt that
perhaps living for Ireland was preferable – and perhaps
more difficult – than dying for her. It also imposed upon
certain families reared in an uncritical republican tradition a kind of responsibility to look for England's difficulty
and continue the struggle. The resurrection of the IRA

at the time of the civil rights agitation of 1968–9 may be directly ascribed to this tradition.

It is difficult to assess whether the result of Easter Week was disastrous for the final settlement of the perennial Irish Question. It hardened unionist attitudes, though some wondered if they could be any harder; it let the British government off the hook, with the sound-hearted but indecisive Asquith having to give place to the brilliant but essentially unsympathetic Lloyd George. He would not confront the absolutism of Carson and Craig and the hot breath of Bonar Law and his baying Conservative and Unionist party reminded him how unrewarding Irish affairs had always been for any British career politician. His reputation for wizardry was at stake and the success of the Treaty negotiations, with the weary Irish delegation unwittingly allowing themselves to be diverted from the hardest nut of all to crack, allowed him to defer the problem of what Churchill memorably metaphorised as 'the dreary steeples of Tyrone and Fermanagh' for later generations to solve.

Yet in spite equally of detractors and interpreters a reappraisal of the men and women of 1916 leaves the researcher with affection if not total approval. It is vain to try to argue that they would have not countenanced the things done in their name; as with most other historical events and personalities later generations reinvent them to suit their own propaganda or psychological needs. They are remembered in Kilmainham, in the Pearse Museum in Rathfarnham and in the 1916 room in the National Museum in Kildare Street. The sight of many personal possessions, Markievicz's Mauser pistol, Pearse's almost unused wig and gown, Connolly's bloodstained shirt (now removed for conservation purposes), all those splendid green uniforms, has a remarkable effect on all but the totally unimaginative. The places associated with Easter Week have a right to their positions as national shrines and a country could have a worse set of revolutionary heroes; there is a lot less painting out of warts required with these than with the equivalents in other countries born in revolt. The line from 'The Mother', possibly Pearse's best known poem, insists upon attention, its ambivalences forgotten:

My sons were faithful, and they fought.

7

RESORT TO ARMS

At Meenbanad, a plateau halfway between Kincasslagh and Dungloe in the Rosses of Donegal, stands a slab monument with the following inscription in Irish and English:

> To commemorate the first action in the War of Independence when the Irish Volunteers rescued two comrades James Ward and James Duffy from British Troops at this place on the 4th day of January 1918.

'This place' was then the last railway halt (known officially as Kincasslagh Road) before the terminus of the Londonderry and Lough Swilly Railway at Burtonport, and the volunteers were removed from the train that was to take them to Derry Jail. The action, carried out by a party of local men that included Fergus Ward and the brothers Dom and John Bonner, antedated by a year and seventeen days the incident that is conventionally regarded as the beginning of the Anglo-Irish War. It was the first of several indications that constitutional methods of achieving the aim of 'old Ireland free' were being thrust aside by the residual Irish Volunteers, soon to call them-

selves the Irish Republican Army. Unlike the majority of
later incidents, it was bloodless – in sharp contrast to the
action at Soloheadbeg, County Tipperary, that resulted in
the point-blank shooting of two Catholic policemen who
were supervising the transport of gelignite to a quarry.
This raid, carried out by nine Volunteers, including Dan
Breen and Seán Treacy, on 21 January 1919, illustrated the
daring and ruthlessness of the Volunteers and marked out
members of the Royal Irish Constabulary as the 'enemy'
– or the most vulnerable part of it. Like the Meenbanad
operation, the Soloheadbeg raid was carried out on local
initiative, without sanction from either the Volunteers'
central command or Dáil Éireann, the intricately linked
parliament which had already formed an alternative system of government.

The RIC had been created as a paramilitary, well-armed
force in 1836 (it was called 'royal' from 1867, because of its
success in fighting Fenianism) but by the later decades of
the nineteenth century it had become essentially a civil
constabulary. By 1919 it had many long-serving Catholics,
most of them nationalists, and was not equipped to fight
a guerrilla war. Its members were conscious, too, that, whatever the outcome of the protracted political process, their
days as a force were numbered; uncertainty about the
future did not help morale. The other Irish constabulary,
the Dublin Metropolitan Police (DMP), had been formed

the same year as the RIC, but the members of the DMP prided themselves on being unarmed – and taller and grander than the other force. By the time the truce was – in some cases reluctantly – agreed, on 9 July 1921, and came into effect on 11 July, the numbers of those killed comprised 428 police (of which ten were DMP officers), 150 military and 750 IRA and civilians.

This last category is necessarily blurred since it included not only active service Volunteers and, to use the modern euphemism, 'collateral' casualties but also at least a hundred people that the local IRA commanders designated, often unjustly, as 'spies'. The 'collaterals' included those caught in crossfire, those who had 'failed to halt when challenged' by military or police patrols and, in a few fearsome cases, women and children. The guerrilla war was an often squalid and violent affair, as is inevitably the case with such struggles: participants ruthlessly acted out the logic of their aims; gallantry to defeated enemies was, with rare exceptions, unknown; and reprisals were often out of all proportion to the original events that had triggered them. Life tended to be regarded as cheap: had not millions, including 50,000 Irish nationals, been killed in the previous half-dozen years? Those involved, except for long-serving members of the RIC – mainly young men – found it necessary to stifle normal human feelings; these feelings finally found their outlet in incredulous dismay at the savagery of their opponents and in self-exculpatory accounts, both oral and written, composed by participants on both sides long after the time of the actual events.

On the Volunteer side, ancient rage and revenge often caused wanton violence against some 'innocents' who were dimly perceived as being 'on the other side', and the war was used to settle personal grudges as well as to ease an atavistic sense of injustice. The crown forces, especially the newly created 'Black and Tans' and the even more ruthless 'Auxiliaries', treated the whole population as hostile, and many unarmed civilians were killed in cold blood. Though called a war of independence, the conflict's primary purpose was rendered *de facto* unachievable by the elections held in May 1921, under the Government of Ireland Act (1920): Ireland was partitioned, and any victory obtained by a continuation of the frightfulness of the war would therefore be incomplete. It was the realisation of this denial of the ultimate ideal that eventually caused the more implacable Volunteers to consider turning from the battlefield to the negotiating table.

The roots of the conflict lay in the British government's attitude to the idea of Irish self-government. Britain had shown a mixture of partiality towards and fear of the unionists from the time of Asquith's Home Rule bill and the signing of the Ulster Covenant in 1912, and had eventually allowed the unionists to control a section of the country that would be politically independent and, with generous subsidies, financially viable. The resulting partition created a state that compromised the northern counties Antrim, Armagh, Derry, Down, Fermanagh and Tyrone, with a built-in, permanent unionist majority and an equally permanent condition of second-class citizenship for three-quarters of a million nationalists whose homes were in Northern Ireland, as partitioned Ulster was now termed. (Northern Ireland also excluded the considerable Protestant populations of Donegal, Monaghan and Cavan.) The remaining twenty-six counties had been offered such a diluted 'independence' that the words 'home rule' were risible, so that even the conservative Catholic hierarchy refused it. The final rejection of the etiolate proposals of Lloyd George, the British prime minister, was caused by the resounding defeat in the post-war election of the party that had been led by John Redmond until his death on 6 March 1918. He, the heir of O'Connell and Parnell, had done everything he could by constitutional methods to achieve the goal of all Irish leaders since the Act of Union (1801): legislative independence.

The need for the preservation of the union had exercised the minds of most British (and all Conservative) statesmen since the time of Sir Robert Peel (1788–1850). (It was his name, first associated with the early constabulary, the Peace Preservation Force in 1814, that caused

the RIC to be known universally as 'Peelers'.) He believed
that, endlessly troublesome as Ireland was (except for the
loyal counties of the north-east), this was a small price to
pay for the maintenance of the integrity of the growing
empire. By the time of the death of the queen in 1901, at
the height of Britain's imperial power, the most that even
the most liberal politician would contemplate was some kind
of weak dominion status for the still-unassimilable Irish.
The Great War – and the Easter Rising – changed everything. A significant number of members of Sinn Féin, the
group which had replaced Redmond's Irish Parliamentary
Party, wanted nothing less than a republic 'virtually established', to use the words of the old IRB oath. The Rising
had shaken the government and, though conscious that
Ireland was the focus of much world attention, especially
from the USA, British politicians, even such Liberals as
Asquith, made no attempt to conceal their distaste for these
nationalist demands.

What increased these politicians' spleen and blunted
their normal political acumen was their need to continue
a war that they were not winning and which was to cost
an enormous number of lives. The principle of 'England's
difficulty; Ireland's opportunity' they saw as heinously dis-
loyal, though to the veterans of the Easter Rising and the
steadily increasing numbers of the Volunteers it was a
simple fact. The movement had recovered quickly from

its disarray after the Rising; in some parts of the country, particularly Munster, there was a continuity of arming and public drilling which brought nationalists into conflict with the police and army. Insensitivity or bloody-mindedness on the part of Lloyd George's government, which was harried by demands from the generals for more soldiers, sharply increased anti-British feeling. The funeral on 25 September 1917 of Thomas Ashe (1885–1917), the hero of the Ashbourne action in Easter Week, who died from pneumonia following forced feeding in Mountjoy Jail, was the occasion of the largest nationalist demonstration seen since Daniel O'Connell's monster meeting at Tara.

The proposal in April 1918 to apply conscription to Ireland, followed by the appointment of the hardline Viscount French as lord lieutenant on 11 May 1918, amounted almost to incitement. The logical result of appointing an army general as viceroy is martial law. Lloyd George tried to mitigate the measure by the offer of the immediate implementation of the Home Rule terms that Redmond had agreed to postpone at the outbreak of the war. This offer was manifestly insincere, since it had no unionist support and by now promised too little to have any persuasive force with the rest of the country. French's announcement, made about a week later, that Sinn Féin were in league with the Germans was not even believed by his predecessor, but a hundred leading Volunteers, including de Valera and

Arthur Griffith, were arrested on 17–18 May. The effect of this was to unite nationalist Ireland as never before – and to shift the balance of power in nationalist Ireland to the militants. The anti-conscription campaign was fought by all nationalists groups, with the strong support of the church and the trade unions, and was eventually successful. The measure (and the promise of Home Rule) was dropped on 20 June, by which time many counties in the west and south were, on French's instructions, under at least partial martial law.

Volunteer tactics required repression for them to succeed; and for the next three years the IRA (as it is convenient to call the military arm of Sinn Féin) and the security forces were in an ironic way collaborators. Ambushes followed by disproportionate reprisals, expressions of national cultural and political will frustrated by draconian oppression, the reputation of both police and army besmirched by gross breaches of discipline – all increased the support for violent tactics. The country which had in general mocked where it did not deplore the 1916 rebels now found itself countenancing much greater violence and tolerating what they would a little earlier have regarded as degraded and criminal. The leaders of the Volunteers, most notably Michael Collins and Cathal Brugha, knew precisely what a guerrilla war entailed and there is a kind of domino inevitability about the sequence of events which led to the struggle for the partial independence that was finally obtained.

It is tempting to think that, because things happened the way they did, no other sequence was possible. In fact there were several possibilities for a more peaceful solution to be reached but a significant number of the new men on the nationalist side were convinced that nothing but a resort to arms would bring the British to their senses. It was an old and a recurring argument, but in this case there existed the will and the means to carry it out – and the necessarily obtuse enemy. Collins had little experience of politics (though he was learning fast) but he was a master of intelligence and the planning of guerrilla tactics. He knew too that, in a country where men were sent to prison for singing seditious songs or giving their names in Irish when accosted by policemen, where there were already easily mobilised local bands of armed zealots and where too long a sacrifice had made a stone of the heart, a war could be started. What he was not sure of was whether it could be finished, or if a majority could stomach what such a war might mean.

The results of the general election in December 1918 were significant not only at home in Ireland – where Sinn Féin secured 73 out of the 105 Irish seats and the old Home Rule party, now led by John Dillon (1851–1927), only six – but also at Westminster, where Lloyd George was returned as head of a coalition dependent on the unionists, led by Bonar Law (1858–1923). The latter had promised total support for Ulster Unionists as early as 1912 and now he left the Welshman with little room to manoeuvre. Lloyd George was inclined to temporise politically while making no effort to stop the spread of martial law and the increasing harassment of ordinary Irish people. Yet, though the extremists would have liked to take the Sinn Féin electoral victory as a licence to proceed with a military campaign, many party members had not given up the hope of a constitutional settlement. The party was even regarded among the ordinary people as the best insurance against renewed violence.

Sinn Féin had been founded in 1905 by Arthur Griffith and Bulmer Hobson (1883–1969), a County Down Quaker, as a means of obtaining a kind of independence, by which Ireland should be an equal partner in a dual monarchy under the English crown. The means of obtaining this solution to the perennial Irish question were to be passive resistance and the setting up of alternative institutions to the existing British ones. (The Irish words *sinn féin* mean 'ourselves'.) This approach met with little practical success but its ideas were wrongly assumed by the authorities to be the philosophical basis for the Easter Rising. It was actually the British who reinvigorated the party, by labelling all activists as Sinn Féiners, and contributed to its election success by their betrayal of John Redmond. In fact Sinn Féin members ranged across the whole spectrum of politics and many disapproved of the growing power of the militarists.

Some, particularly de Valera, pinned their hopes on the Paris Peace Conference, which was due to open on 20 January 1919 to consider the rights of 'small nations'. The dominating figure at the conference was to be the American president, Woodrow Wilson (1856–1924), who was assumed, as a Democrat, to be sympathetic to nationalist aspirations. Considering the resolute Presbyterianism of his County Tyrone grandparents and his own instinctive Waspishness, this was an incorrect assumption: Wilson, though happy to be made a freeman of Dublin on 3 January, was clearly reluctant to do anything about a matter that the British delegation insisted was 'internal'. All the members of Sinn Féin, of whatever colour, were determined upon independence and logically set up Dáil Éireann, an independent government that intended to send an independent delegation to Paris (with no success, as it turned out). The president of this government was de Valera, with Collins in charge of finance and Brugha responsible for defence. De Valera was still in jail because of the 'German Plot' and Brugha presided when the Dáil met for the first time on 21 January in the Mansion House in Dawson Street, Dublin. By then, although it was not realised by anyone, the war for independence was two days old, and it had not been declared by Sinn Féin.

8

TARGETS

Seán Treacy, the leader of the Soloheadbeg ambush, had initiated the war for independence because, as he put it, 'it was high time we did a bit of pushing.' Dan Breen gave a more sober version of events: 'The Volunteers were in great danger of becoming merely a political adjunct to the Sinn Féin organisation'. The nine participants were local: both Breen and Treacy lived close to the quarry to which the 168 pounds of gelignite and thirty-eight detonators were being conveyed by horse and cart from the military barracks in Tipperary. Two RIC constables, fifty-seven-year-old James McDonnell, a married man from County Mayo, and thirty-six-year-old Patrick O'Donnell, a bachelor from County Cork, were sent along as guards with the driver, Patrick Godfrey. They were met at the entrance to the quarry by the county council employee, Patrick Flynn, who was to take delivery. The constables fell dead in a hail of rifle and revolver shots, and, in the confusion of collecting the police rifles and gelignite, Breen's mask slipped, thus enabling the authorities to use his photograph on reward posters offering £1,000 for information leading to his capture.

Though it was the first – and an entirely unauthorised – action in the struggle, this episode shared one feature with other similar attacks: local intelligence was of good quality. The South Tipperary Brigade were told that a consignment of explosives would 'soon be on its way to the quarry' and so the ambush party was in position on each day from dawn on 16 January, leaving the scene around 2 p.m. in the afternoon. Local and national reaction was one of almost universal condemnation. The constables had been popular members of a small-town community; a relief fund for McDonnell's family (he left a wife and five children) was set up immediately. The local clergy and Dr Harty, the archbishop of Cashel, declared the action morally wrong. It was also condemned by Sinn Féin and leading members of the IRB, though whether the disapproval by these last two was of the action or its freelance nature is unclear. Certainly *An tÓglach*, the IRB journal edited by Piaras Beaslaí, announced on 31 January that Volunteers were entitled morally and politically to inflict death on the enemies of the state: 'soldiers and policemen of the British Government'.

The next RIC casualty was Constable Martin O'Brien, who was shot on 6 April during an attempt by a Limerick City company of the IRA to rescue Robert Byrne, a republican hunger striker, from St Camillus' Hospital. Like south Tipperary after Soloheadbeg and Westport after the shooting of a magistrate on 31 March, the area was proclaimed a military area. Though all these deaths were greeted with genuine revulsion, the swamping of the areas with military and police checkpoints, the humiliating body searches, the requirement of permits for journeys or even the driving of stock to market and the general interference with ordinary life soon blunted the regret. It seemed that the British government had learned nothing, not even the wisdom of allowing the local and generally tactful RIC to continue to maintain order.

The Soloheadbeg team went into action again on 13 May, rescuing Seán Hogan from the Thurles–Cork train at Knocklong station, just over the county boundary in Limerick. As a result of the action, Sergeant Peter Wallace and Constable Michael Enright died from gunshot wounds and Breen himself was so severely wounded that he was not expected to survive. Again there was strong condemnation of the shootings, with Dr Harty denouncing the action and urging Irishmen 'not to stain the fair name of their native land with deeds of blood'. In all, fifteen policemen were killed in 1919, including a district inspector, Michael Hunt, after the Thurles Races on 23 June. More significantly, two of those who lost their lives were DMP detectives: DS Patrick Smyth (killed on 30 July) and DC

Daniel Hoey (12 September). These were part of the city police force's G-Division, the plain-clothes members of which were called G-men (long before the members of J. Edgar Hoover's FBI were known by the same name). They were the first victims of Collins' deadly band of counter-intelligence operatives, known as 'the Squad'.

Collins was enough of a student of Irish history to realise that, in all previous Irish insurrections – that of the United Irishmen in 1798, Robert Emmet's in 1803, William Smith O'Brien's in 1848 and the Fenian outbreak in 1867 – government intelligence agents had discovered the details of plans and personnel well in advance of the attack. He was determined to reverse this situation by building up his own network of spies and counter-intelligence operatives. The Squad was essentially a band of expert gunmen officially formed in September 1919, though a notional Squad existed before that. Dick McKee, one of Collins' chief aides, who helped train them, had warned prospective members that those with scruples about taking life should not join.

DS Smyth was a very effective detective, known as 'Dog' Smyth because of his sleuthing ability. Like many G-men, he had been warned by some of Collins' men that he should be less assiduous in his work but he persisted and was shot by five gunmen having alighted from a tram at Drumcondra Bridge. He returned fire and managed to reach his home before collapsing. DC Hoey had been an intended target of Collins ever since he had picked out Seán MacDermott (1884–1916), one of the leaders of the 1916 Rising, from the crowd of Volunteers who were to be shipped to the relative safety of an English prison. MacDermott was executed in Kilmainham on 12 May 1916 and the name of Hoey was filed away in Collins' prodigious memory for future action. Hoey was shot as he entered the police station in Brunswick Street on the day that the government proscribed Dáil Éireann.

One of Collins' most effective Castle spies was Ned Broy. He had joined the DMP in 1911 and served as a sergeant-clerk in G-division. His usual technique was to slip an extra carbon and flimsy into his typewriter for every document he dealt with and pass the copy to Collins later that evening. It was from Broy that Collins got the list of those whom the government intended to arrest because of the 'German Plot'. As a result, Collins was able to warn de Valera and the rest of the Volunteer Executive at their meeting on 17 May 1918 that they were likely to be arrested. For reasons that can be guessed, de Valera went home; a few days later he found himself a prisoner in Lincoln Jail. His rescue from prison on 3 February 1919 became part of the Collins legend, with all the ripping-yarns paraphernalia of keys made from wax impressions which broke in the lock and the prisoner walking arm in arm with one of his rescuers past groups of courting Tommies and their sweethearts.

De Valera was the obvious leader of the Irish forces: he was a veteran of Easter Week, probably the most successful military commander on the Irish side and a politician with a remarkably supple, not to say Machiavellian, mind. He was famous for recommending Richard Mulcahy, the Volunteer chief of staff, to read *Il Principe*, and ever since the Rising he had shown a distrust of violence. He was also immovable once he had made a decision. Instead of staying at home to organise the 'war' that was brewing, he insisted on going to America. The decision caused the rest of the Executive some dismay, especially those, like Griffith (released in the general amnesty in March), who wished to hold the militant wing of Sinn Féin in check. In fact, de Valera leaving left Collins free to conduct the war as he saw fit. He knew the propaganda and morale-boosting value of the 'spectacular' to complement the series of raids and ambushes being carried on by individual IRA brigades and it seemed to him that the most spectacular action might be the successful assassination of the viceroy. John French had gone to his home in Roscommon and was on his way back to Dublin on 19 December. An ambush was laid near the viceregal lodge in Phoenix Park but the only casualty was a Volunteer named Savage who was caught in crossfire. When, on 21 December, the *Irish Independent* described Savage as 'a would-be assassin', the paper's offices and presses were destroyed by a party of Volunteers.

Action was not confined to the IRA: at least some attempt was made at setting up Griffith's counter-state. As well as being virtual commander of operations, Collins was minister of finance in the Dáil, and he raised £380,000 in redeemable bonds repayable by the future independent Ireland. (He also discovered during the flotation that most ordinary people are slow to part with money for any cause.) Sinn Féin soon controlled so many councils as to give them control of local government. Rates were no longer paid and arbitration courts, whose decisions were binding, were preferred to the state ones. There was even an attempt made to set up a Sinn Féin police force. This 'dry-run' at self-government increased confidence sufficiently that post-Treaty Ireland was governed with an unexpected efficiency.

9

BLACK AND TANS – AND AUXIES

The year 1920 began with the ominous arrival in Ireland of the new RIC recruits, intended to supplement the native Irish force, which was then reeling from IRA attacks and social ostracism. The total numbers who left the force in 1919 for all causes was 495, of which only 99 had resigned. The equivalent figures for 1920 were 3,229, with almost exactly half that number of resignations and 178 killed in action. The order for supplementary recruitment was issued on 2 January and by 21 November 1921 the force's numbers had reached 9,500. The personnel were ex-soldiers and ex-sailors who, unemployed and finding life dull after the excitement of the war, were happy to become mercenaries for ten shillings a day and all-found. The urgency was such that complete uniforms could not be found for the first draft. They wore dark green police hats and belts over khaki uniforms and made no attempt to hide their military nature. They first appeared on patrol in Upper Church, County Tipperary, where there was a famous local pack of hounds called the 'Black and Tans'; the name was applied to the new recruits and it stuck. In spite of the equally foul reputation of the Auxiliary cadets, who were first recruited in July 1920, the struggle of 1920–21 became known as the 'Tan war'.

In spite of contemporary belief, the vetting process at recruitment was nearly as strict as for ordinary RIC officers. There may have been some few with a criminal record but most were young men who were only too happy to engage in the reprisals that were at first condoned and eventually openly approved by the increasingly desperate authorities. The 'sweepings of English jails' – the usual nationalist jibe – was an inaccurate description but many of the exploits of the new recruits were criminal if viewed in absolute terms. They were badly trained and, apart from the perhaps one-quarter of them who were native Irish recruits, had no experience or knowledge of the country in which they found themselves. Even the Irish recruits, who were mainly of Ulster origin, would have found Munster and west Connacht, the main places of deployment outside of Dublin, somewhat alien. The force's pied appearance did not last; by the end of 1920 uniforms were again uniform and it was impossible to tell the strangers from the regular RIC, except by accent and, some would say, by behaviour.

In fact the first piece of serious breach of police discipline took place before the 'Tans' were mobilised. On 22 January twenty-nine-year-old Constable Michael Finnegan was walking home to the Mall in Thurles when he was shot by three men. The local police immediately went on the rampage, shooting out the windows of twelve prominent Sinn Féiners and throwing grenades through the office window of the *Tipperary Star*. This action was on a small scale compared with later excesses. The day before the Thurles incident, the Squad had struck at their most senior target: William Redmond, the assistant commissioner of the DMP, who had been put in charge of the demoralised G Division, was shot in the back as he walked from the Castle to his hotel in Harcourt Street.

On the night of 19–20 March, after the shooting of Constable Joseph Murtagh in Pope's Quay, Cork, a band of armed men with blackened faces and in civilian clothes burst into the home of Tomás MacCurtain, the Sinn Féin lord mayor of the city. They rushed straight upstairs and shot him. The inquest returned a verdict of wilful murder against 'David Lloyd George, Prime Minister of England, Lord French, Lord Lieutenant of Ireland, Ian MacPherson, Late Chief Secretary of Ireland, Acting Inspector General Smith of the RIC, Divisional Inspector Clayton of the RIC, DI Swanzy and some unknown members of the RIC'. The authorities tried to say that the perpetrators had been members of the IRB, who were impatient at MacCurtain's lack of support for the campaign, but no one believed the story. Swanzy was placed on Collins' mental list of enemies to be eliminated; he was shot in Lisburn, County Antrim, on 22 August. The aftermath was serious sectarian rioting in Lisburn and Belfast. Most Catholic houses in Lisburn were destroyed and there were twenty-four civilian deaths. These riots, together with the even more savage ones in Derry earlier in the summer, led to the recruitment of men for the Ulster Special Constabularies; the most notorious of these, the 'B' Specials, manned by part-time loyalists, were to continue as a notably partial force until their final disbandment in 1970.

The shock of MacCurtain's death and the evidence of RIC involvement in the crime was mitigated somewhat by the killing by the Squad of Alan Bell on 26 March. Bell was an elderly magistrate who was part of French's counter-espionage team. He was known to have been successful in finding evidence of Sinn Féin bank accounts. He used to travel each day by tram from his home in Monkstown without a guard. That morning four members of the Squad took him off the tram at Ballsbridge and shot him. Another high-profile incident had a less bloody conclusion. General Lucas was captured by an IRA platoon led by Liam Lynch (1893–1923) while fishing on the Blackwater, near Fermoy, County Cork, on 26 July. He was moved around for a month until his guard, Michael Brennan, tired of sup-plying him with a daily bottle of whiskey paid for out of Brennan's own pocket, allowed him to escape. Relations between the general and his captors were genial; he played tennis, made hay and wrote and received daily letters from his wife. They took him salmon poaching one night and he was relieved to see that the IRA boatman was the river bailiff. On the darker side, the general's troops went on the rampage in Fermoy and other towns in reprisal for the kidnapping, although, unlike in Tan and Auxiliary raids, no one was killed.

The Auxies – the Auxiliary Division of the RIC – were the brainchild of Winston Churchill, minister of war and the air in Lloyd George's coalition. They were ex-British army officers and, with permission to wear either army uniform (without insignia) or police uniform, they were literally 'Black and Tan'; their distinguishing feature was the wearing of Glengarry bonnets. Later they had distinctive blue uniforms with black chest bandoliers and leather belts holding bayonets and open holsters with .45 revolvers. Most had been high-ranking officers and many had been decorated for valour, including two holders of the VC and many DSOs, MCs and holders of the Croix de Guerre. Their reputation in Ireland, however, was of drunkenness, brutality and lack of discipline, to the extent that their commander, General Frank Crozier, resigned on 19 February 1921, a mere six and a half months after taking command. They were meant as quick-response, motorised units of a hundred men whose targets were the newly organised IRA flying squads, which operated mainly in Munster.

The most notorious examples of reprisals were the 'sackings' of various Irish towns. Typical was the Auxiliary action in Balbriggan, County Dublin, on 20 September 1920. Head Constable Peter Burke and his brother Michael, a sergeant, were shot with dum-dum bullets in a public house. Peter died on the spot but Michael later recovered from his wounds. Peter had been involved in training the Auxiliary Division in the Phoenix Park depot. A party of Auxiliaries arrived from Gormanston and, on seeing, it is said, their old instructor lying dead, wreaked destruction on property with grenades, setting many houses on fire and savagely killing two civilians with bayonets. The scene was marked by lines of refugees fleeing from their ravaged town. From this time the beleaguered inhabitants of towns and villages where reprisals were expected took to leaving their homes at sundown and spending the night in what safety they could find in hedges and barns. Similar scenes followed the killing of a sergeant and five constables at Rineen, between Milltown Malbay and Lahinch, County Clare, the next day. Houses were burnt in the nearby towns and four people were killed, including one who tried to help a neighbour put out the fire in his house. On 28 September Liam Lynch and Ernie O'Malley (1898–1957) captured the RIC barracks in Mallow, County Cork. During the raid an army sergeant was killed, and later that evening the army ravaged the town. Two days later it was the turn of Trim, County Meath, when the town was wrecked and the shops looted by Tans after the RIC barracks was set on fire by the IRA.

10

BLOODY SUNDAY

The autumn of 1920 and the spring of 1921 were to prove the bloodiest periods of the war. They were characterised by attacks on barracks, now fortified by barbed wire and sandbags, as well as ambushes, reprisals and counter-reprisals, intimidation and physical violence inflicted by both sides on civilians, and a swift descent into terror for the parts of the country where there was IRA activity. The cities of Cork, Limerick and Dublin and the counties of Cork, Tipperary, Kerry, Limerick, Clare, Roscommon and Donegal bore the brunt of the fighting. Yet even there, large areas were unaffected, except by dread and rumour, and the inconvenience of military restrictions. Between January 1919 and the Truce in July 1921 there were 136 recorded IRA operations in Cork but the north of the county was relatively quiet; Tipperary had fifty-eight, Kerry forty-four, Limerick thirty-three, Clare twenty-five and Donegal eleven. Thirty-nine policemen were killed in Ulster, eight in Belfast and four in Derry, with the remainder mainly in the border regions of Armagh, Cavan, Monaghan and Donegal. One was a head constable and seven were 'specials' who had been commissioned after November 1920. IRA activity was generally light in the north until 1922 but attacks on police continued there after the Truce and the setting up of the Northern Ireland state in June 1921. Between then and the time of the death of the last recorded casualty, Special Constable Samuel Hayes, who was shot in the Newtownards Road, Belfast on 5 August, seven officers were killed.

Though official sanction for reprisals was not given until January 1922, there was little attempt at investigating those responsible for the indiscriminate killing of civilians. After Balbriggan, Sir Hamar Greenwood, the chief secretary, who had been appointed on 4 April 1920 and whose public utterances became so specious that 'telling a Hamar' became a euphemism for lying, told the House of Commons that it was 'impossible' to find out who was responsible for the burning, looting and killing. The implicit policy had been baldly stated by Lt Col Brice Smyth, the RIC divisional commander for Munster, at Listowel on 9 June. In an address to a group of RIC officers he urged them to be ruthless: 'The more you shoot the better I will like you, and no policeman will get into trouble for shooting a man.' He also hinted at the vicious treatment that was being meted out to IRA prisoners and, since their purpose was to wipe out Sinn Féin, 'any man who is not prepared to do this is a hindrance, and had better leave the job at once.' One courageous constable did just that: Jeremiah Mee walked up to the table and threw his revolver and cap upon it, saying that Smyth's speech was incitement to murder. Smyth ordered his arrest but nobody moved. The incident became known as the 'Listowel Mutiny' and the highly decorated one-armed veteran was added to Collins' list. Mee and several colleagues resigned on 6 July and Smyth was killed in the smoking-room of the Cork Country Club eleven days later by members of the Cork No. 1 Brigade. Mee was recruited by Collins as a propagandist to tour the United States with tales of the government policy of atrocity – ironically, as it now seems, since Collins' policy was not notably different from the government's.

Major George Smyth, who was then serving in Egypt, on hearing of the death of his brother applied for a transfer to Irish intelligence, bringing with him, it is said, eleven comrades for the sole intention of avenging the killing, which he blamed, incorrectly, on Dan Breen. Breen and Treacy had been active in Dublin since the failed attempt on French's life in which they had taken part; they were doughty fighters and Collins wanted to keep them under his direct control. The arrival of Smyth in Dublin coincided with the effective reorganisation of government intelligence by Brig. Gen. Sir Ormonde Winter, known to the Squad as the 'Holy Terror'. His agents had located Breen and Treacy at a house in Whitehall. In the raid which took place on 10 October, Smyth and another officer were killed, and the householder, Professor John Carolan of St Patrick's Training College, put against the wall and shot in the head, but the two Volunteers, in spite of serious wounds, escaped. The funeral of Smyth, fixed for 14 October, was expected to be a solemn affair, with General Neville Macready (British commander in chief since April) and General Henry Tudor (commander of the RIC) in attendance. It was too good an opportunity for Collins to miss. The Squad, with Treacy among them, attended but, probably on Winter's advice, the generals stayed away. Treacy was recognised in the doorway of the Republican Outfitters, run by Dublin IRA officer Peadar Clancy, and was shot during a raid. Major Smyth's body was taken to Banbridge, County Down, to be buried in the family plot beside his brother.

Two other 'names' of Volunteer mythology were to die that autumn: Terence MacSwiney, who had succeeded MacCurtain as lord mayor of Cork, died on 25 October after seventy-four days on hunger strike; and Kevin Barry, an eighteen-year-old medical student, was hanged for being in possession of a gun at the scene of the killing of an even younger soldier on 20 September. Barry bequeathed one of the long-surviving ballads of the period ('Another martyr for old Ireland; another murder for the crown') and MacSwiney set a pattern for future republicans.

Both deaths increased the surge of world opinion against Britain. The *Manchester Guardian* and the *Daily News* (whose literary editor, Robert Lynd, had been a member of the original Sinn Féin and a friend of Roger Casement) attacked the government constantly, effectively neutralising the rabid anti-Irish propaganda of the *Morning Post* and the *Spectator*. The most telling propaganda sheet was the *Irish Bulletin*, put out by Desmond Fitzgerald (1889–1947), Frank Gallagher and Erskine Childers. The *Bulletin* had even more impact abroad than at home. Its experienced journalists – Childers had written the bestselling *The Riddle of the Sands* (1903), which anticipated Germany's entry into the Great War – were able to depict Volunteer successes as heroic and condemn government actions as squalidly savage. As a result of such publicity, de Valera was able to win a great deal of sympathy in America for the Irish cause – as well as securing $5 million for use in Ireland. Lloyd George was no longer able to close his eyes and wish the Irish problem would go away.

The worst month of 1920 proved to be November; it was in fact probably the worst month in the whole struggle. In the early morning of 21 November the Squad killed eleven members of the British secret service in their homes and hotels. Two Auxiliaries, Frank Garniss and Cecil Morris, who happened to be on the scene of one of the killings in Lower Mount Street, were themselves killed; they were the first Auxiliary fatalities. Two of Collins' closest aides, Dick McKee and Peadar Clancy, who had been arrested the previous evening, were 'shot while trying to escape'. So 'Bloody Sunday' began. It was the day of a football final between Dublin and Tipperary, and Croke Park was crowded that afternoon. The grounds were surrounded by crown forces in the likely anticipation of their finding Volunteers among the crowd. Against instructions, a party of Auxiliaries drove into the ground while the match was in progress. Predictably, they claimed they had been fired on from the crowd; what is certain is that they turned their guns on the teams and shot into the stands. Twelve people died – some from bullets, others trampled to death as the hysterical crowd tried to find cover. The fatalities included a woman, a child and one of the Tipperary forwards.

These events, which in a sense cancelled each other out in terms of their horror, received worldwide publicity, thus edging Lloyd George, with infinite slowness, towards tentative moves to a truce. These moves stopped again when, one week later, Tom Barry's West Cork flying column ambushed an Auxiliary patrol at Kilmichael. The cadets were under the command of DI F. W. Crake and travelled in two Crossley tenders on their usual triangular sweep:

Macroom, Dunmanway, Bandon and back to Macroom. Barry had begun training his men on Bloody Sunday and chose a stretch of bogland near Kilmichael, eight miles from Macroom. Eighteen Auxiliaries were killed – some by Mills bombs and others, it was insisted by the government information offices, after they had surrendered. There were accusations, too, of mutilations of the bodies of the dead using axes and of the stealing of personal possessions. Barry himself said that all the dead had been killed in the fighting and that the Auxiliaries had used a favourite trick of the false surrender, which had resulted in the deaths of two Volunteers.

A reprisal, perhaps the most notorious of all, came two weeks later, on Saturday 11 December, when, after an ambush at Dillon's Cross in Cork in which an Auxiliary was killed and ten of his companions wounded, the centre of the city was set on fire by a combined force of drunken Tans and Auxiliaries. They prevented the fire service from reaching the sites of many of the blazes and looted what they could from the burning stores. Afterwards Auxiliaries swaggered around Dublin with burnt corks on their Glengarries. Greenwood had to tell another 'Hamar' in the House, claiming, with enviable effrontery, that the city had been torched by its own citizens. The report of the military enquiry undertaken by General Strickland, the OC for the Cork district, was never published because its effect 'would be disastrous to the government's whole policy in Ireland'. Three million pounds was paid later in compensation.

Lloyd George was out to please his audience when he claimed at the yearly Guildhall banquet in the City of London on 9 November: 'We have murder by the throat'. He used the occasion to exonerate those crown forces who were guilty of excesses in Ireland and gave a hint that they should be given a freer rein in the future. His suggestion of an official sanction for reprisals and the treating of the Volunteers as criminals was also to please his minister of defence, Winston Churchill, who, though a Liberal since 1906, was already giving clear indications of his intention to rejoin the Tory party of his 'Orange card'-playing father, Lord Randolph (1849–95). It was Churchill who insisted that Kevin Barry be hanged as a murderer and who prompted J. H. Thomas, who was afterwards to be dominions minister in Ramsay MacDonald's first Labour government, to condemn the execution in the House.

Lloyd George knew that, if the killings by the IRA were murders, then so too were those carried out by his forces in Ireland. There was a deal of semantic shuffling as to what was the exact nature of the crimes of the IRA. They insisted – and truly believed – that they were fighting a glorious war finally to free Ireland from English rule and that they were right to declare Ireland as a 'virtually established' republic. Yet it would have been 'dignifying the action of murderers' for the government to elevate the IRA's guerrilla activity to the level of legitimate conflict – despite the fact that such a recognition would have given the army generals a freer hand in dealing with insurgents. As it was, the generals continually felt themselves shackled by political restraints; even the go-ahead for 'official' reprisals contained implicit conditions.

The horrors of the year were not over yet: Canon Magner, parish priest of Dunmanway and a young parishioner of his, Timothy Crowley, were shot dead by an Auxiliary officer on 15 December because the priest had not tolled his church bells on Armistice Day. This happened exactly a month after the body of Fr Michael Griffin, a priest from Barna, County Galway, with known Volunteer sympathies, had been found riddled with bullets near his home the day after his arrest by crown forces. Nineteen twenty headed towards its murky close with two incidents that were entirely characteristic of its terror. On 27 December the RIC carried out a raid on a big house, left vacant by its owners, at Bruff, County Limerick, where a dance was being held to raise funds for the East Limerick Third Battalion of the IRA. Five IRA men were shot and seventeen injured, and two Tans were killed in the assault. Then, on 29 December, three Tans on patrol in Midleton, County Cork, were shot; they eventually died of their injuries. The town was to be the scene of the first 'official reprisal' by soldiers on 1 January 1921, when seven houses were destroyed. Another year of apparently endless violence had begun.

11

TRUCE

The last six months of the war were its bloodiest and most squalid: the number of police casualties from January to July was 235 – 57 more than for the whole of 1920; 707 civilians were killed and 756 wounded. Of the civilians killed, more than a hundred were shot by the IRA as spies – a term that often meant refusal to cooperate with the local brigade, as when a labourer was shot for filling in a trench dug by local Volunteers. An even greater number were deliberately shot by crown forces. Young men were particularly at risk from Tans and Auxiliaries, whose lack of discipline and lawlessness eventually caused the latter's commander, Brig. Gen. Frank Crozier, to resign on 19 February after his dismissals had been overruled by General Tudor, the head of police. His rejection of them as 'a drunken and insubordinate body of men' was no surprise to the people of Ireland and was officially ignored by the government. Yet it was another blow against Lloyd George's conduct of Irish affairs and a further stimulus to the moves to seek some cessation of the violence.

Female fatalities, till then the result of being caught in crossfire, now happened as part of raids. On 14 May 1921 DI Harry Biggs and the daughter of Sir Charles Barrington were killed on the way home from a fishing expedition at Newport, County Tipperary; two other women and an army officer escaped unharmed. The next day DI Blake and his wife were killed (she was shot five times) when their car was ambushed coming home from a tennis match at Gort, County Galway. (The number of police fatalities for that May – fifty-six – was the greatest for any month of the conflict.) The incident that caused the greatest revulsion was the kidnapping and shooting of an elderly woman, Mrs Lindsay, who had reported to the authorities that an ambush was being prepared near her home at Coachford, County Cork. On foot of the information she passed on, seven IRA men were apprehended and executed in Cork on 5 February; that same evening six unarmed soldiers were killed in Cork city.

IRA ambushes (the numbers of the ambush parties often heavily outnumbering their targets) and individual assassinations continued as did Tan and Auxiliary raids. On 7 March the Sinn Féin mayor of Limerick, George Clancy, former mayor Michael O'Callaghan and Joseph O'Donoghue were shot dead in their homes, almost a year after Tomás MacCurtain had been dispatched in a similar fashion. There was a half-hearted attempt made to discipline the Tans and Auxiliaries: the 'official' reprisal in Midleton, County Cork, on 1 January was the last of its kind but more and more of the country was placed under martial law.

The presence of de Valera, who had returned from America on 23 December 1920, was beginning to have an effect. He was utterly intractable once he had made a decision and, though it seemed odd that he found it necessary to spend nineteen months away from the racked country, no one, least of all Collins, cared either to try to prevent his going to America or to comment upon the length of his stay there. As ever, de Valera showed a less than noble capacity for making sure he would not be held responsible for hard decisions. He was deeply concerned about the effect that the campaign was having upon the country and rather surprised at the position that Collins had secured for himself. De Valera had little taste for guerrilla fighting; the lack of military uniform, though a considerable advantage for the IRA, meant that there could be no appeal to the Geneva Convention about such things as prisoners' rights. Greenwood had made it clear that the 5,000 internees in camps like Ballykinlar, near Dundrum in County Down, would receive prisoner-of-war treatment without being given POW status.

De Valera's time in America had toughened him politically; he found he was no match for the tough Irish-

American career politicians who, among other things, wished to wreck the League of Nations – Woodrow Wilson's great hope for lasting peace. Wilson, heavily incapacitated in his last months of office by a stroke, was of no help when it came to securing recognition of Ireland's right to independence, and when, in November 1919, the Republican W. G. Harding (1865–1923) was elected president on an isolationist ticket without a single mention of Ireland during his campaign, it was clear that Ireland could expect no official support from America. As Harding said, when asked to support Irish independence, 'I would not care to undertake to say to Great Britain what she must do, any more than I would permit her to tell us what we must do with the Philippines.'

De Valera, with his innate distrust of lawlessness, wanted to set the IRA's activities on a moral basis, regardless of the fact that the lack of such a foundation for their actions did not worry Collins or Brugha (who were now drifting apart), let alone the various brigades. As *príomh-aire* of Dáil Éireann, de Valera was in a position to insist that a formal state of war be declared against Britain and on 11 March the proclamation was made. He urged a cutting-back in IRA activity, as if that were either practicable or popular: 'What we want is one good battle with about 500 men on each side.' Such a 'good battle' actually took place, at his urging, on 25 May, when the Customs House, where many local government records were stored, was occupied and burned by the IRA. Troops and Auxiliaries surrounded the building before the raiding party could escape. Five Volunteers were killed and eighty taken prisoner – and one of Dublin's architectural glories burned for five days. From Collins' point of view the action was a military disaster and did nothing to improve relations between him and de Valera, who were now quite obviously at odds. Yet coming when it did at a time when Lloyd George's government could no longer bear the shadows on its reputation abroad, especially in America, it proved to be a political triumph.

Lloyd George's position within the coalition had not improved, even though one of the hawks had turned into a dove. Churchill, whose political antennae were even more sensitive than de Valera's, came out strongly in favour of a truce. The prime minister's own Liberal Party was now in a minority and dependent on the grace and favour of Arthur Balfour (1848–1930), leader of the Conservatives, and the unionist Bonar Law. Lloyd George also had to face down his often baying, red-faced generals, who always said they could finish the thing if he removed the political constraints under which they operated. Truce negotiations were conducted with all the formality and indecision of a seventeenth-century court minuet. Even as Lloyd George was prating about having 'murder by the throat' he was testing the possibilities of compromise, and many worthy people worked tirelessly to effect a solution. One was the archbishop of Perth, P. J. Clune, whose nephew, a civilian Gaelic Leaguer, had been arrested in the same hotel as McKee and Clancy, and like them had been 'shot while trying to escape'. Clune's efforts failed when Lloyd George refused to deal with the rebels before they gave up their arms – a song that is being heard again!

Negotiations were continued mainly by 'Andy' Cope, who was the joint Irish under-secretary and one of the tireless heroes of the process. The arrest on 22 June of de Valera, who was now president of the second Dáil – which had 124 Sinn Féin members, all elected unopposed – was an embarrassment that Cope had to deal with. De Valera was released the next day. Another nationalist objection to the process was the refusal to allow Collins to be a party to peace talks. Under the Government of Ireland Act, if southern Ireland would not accept an agreed self-government, it would revert to the position of a crown colony, which would have meant the entire twenty-six counties being under martial law; it was reckoned that this would require 100,000 troops to maintain. With no let-up in IRA activity and deafening criticism even from the British newspapers, the pressure to treat eventually became overwhelming. George V's speech at the opening of the Belfast parliament in the City Hall on 22 June, written for him by Lloyd George, with a significant contribution by Jan

Smuts, finally persuaded the British people that the time had come for peace. The king urged 'all Irishmen to pause, to stretch out the hand of forbearance and conciliation, to forgive and forget and to join in making for the land which they love a new era of peace, contentment and goodwill.'

The IRA, especially those members in the south and west, who were by now veteran warriors, were not likely to be impressed by such sentiments, expressed by such a person in such a place on the occasion of the formal partitioning of the country. They were, however, in need of respite: Collins reckoned that resistance could not have continued for more than three weeks. Lloyd George had removed all his previous conditions about personnel and the laying down of arms and, although de Valera was at his most byzantine in terms of the conditions he imposed, a truce concluded in the Mansion House between Macready and his aide Col Brind and Éamonn Duggan and Robert Barton came into effect on 11 July. The conditions included a cessation of attacks on crown forces and civilians, the avoidance of provocative displays of force and no reinforcements of men or arms by either side; the provisions were to apply to the area under martial law as well as the rest of the country.

The truce was fragile but it held. Collins and the other leaders understood the risk the IRA took 'like rabbits coming out of their holes' and many were confused. The last killing was of four unarmed soldiers at 9 p.m. the night before the truce was signed; the last policemen, Constable Alexander Clarke, had been shot that afternoon in Skibbereen. It took some time for the realisation that the country was again at peace to sink in. One slightly cynical, if not unexpected, result of the end of hostilities was the increase in numbers joining the IRA – the 'Trucileers', as the famous and ubiquitous anonymous Irish wit was to call them. Those who had fought in constant danger of their lives on both sides were glad of at least a temporary lull; ominous cracks were already beginning to appear in the smooth façade of IRA unity. No revolution can be entirely bloodless, and worse was to come.

Yet throughout the twenty-six counties there was a light-headed sense that maybe now things would get better. The war had generated plenty of new heroes – Tom Barry, Liam Deasy, Seán Treacy, Dan Breen, Ernie O'Malley, Oscar Traynor, Liam Lynch, Seán MacEoin, and many others whose story was not yet complete. Not all the Volunteers were heroes and not all their adversaries were villains. Some names live in local infamy; some were – and still are – granted a grudging respect. One egregious exception to this was Major Arthur Percival of the Essex regiment, who liked to ride about south Cork in an open car with a loaded gun in his hands, looking for targets. He was undoubtedly responsible for the torture of prisoners and was lucky to escape with his life. He did live to face the humiliation, as Lt General Percival, of surrendering his army to the much smaller Japanese force in Singapore on 15 February 1942 after 'the greatest military defeat in the history of the British Empire'.

When the terms of the truce were published, there followed a week of rioting in Belfast. Members of the new Special Constabulary, mostly recruited from the UVF, joined forces with Protestant mobs over the Twelfth holiday. Sixteen Catholics and seven Protestants were killed and over 200 Catholic homes were destroyed. There was nothing new in anti-Catholic pogroms but the appalled minority nationalist population was beginning to understand what the Government of Ireland Act was to mean to them. The Volunteers and their late adversaries had other things on their minds but the news from the north should have concentrated the minds of the peacemakers. It is, even at this distance, hard to understand why they had so little understanding of the Ulster unionists and why they allowed the promise of a boundary commission to blind their eyes to the real flaw in the treaty terms. The Volunteers were entitled to their moment of triumph; they were yet to learn the truth of the final words of David Neligan, one of Collins' Castle moles, in his book *The Spy in the Castle*: 'Revolution devours her own children'.

12

THE TREATY – AND DOCUMENT NO. 2

The truce which called a stop to open hostilities in the Anglo-Irish War and prepared the way for the negotiation of the treaty which set up the Irish Free State came into effect on 11 July 1921. The war – really a series of localised guerrilla raids, ambushes and brutal reprisals by the Black and Tans and the Auxiliaries – had resulted in the deaths of 428 RIC officers (many of them Catholic), 150 military personnel and an estimated 750 IRA members and civilians. Its causes were both proximate and remote, coming as it did at the end of nearly a decade of crowded political and armed activity, but unquestionably it began because of the end of confidence in Redmondite constitutionalism and the successes of Sinn Féin in the election of 1918, when in a 48 per cent poll they won 73 out of 105 Irish seats.

John Redmond (1856–1918), Parnell's political heir, had managed to unite the Irish party sufficiently again to hold the political balance in the House of Commons in 1912 and to persuade Asquith (1852–1928) to introduce a Home

Rule bill. Like his master, and earlier Daniel O'Connell, Redmond strove to avoid an armed uprising, believing with considerable justification that any such resort would harm Ireland more than its enemy. Like Parnell he underestimated the strength of Ulster Protestants' legitimate fears and the strength of their will to resist Rome Rule. The Ulster Volunteer Force (UVF), founded in 1913 to coordinate paramilitary resistance among northern unionists, was secretly aided by elements in the Conservative party and supported by retired officers of the British army. No attempt was made to prevent the distribution of arms after the Larne gun-running of April 1914, and the Curragh mutiny (March 1914) indicated clearly to the British government that it could not count upon the obedience of some of the senior officers in the army, a number of whom were of Ulster extraction.

Asquith and his cabinet showed little resolve in the face of such historical threats, and the question of whether Ulster would resort to 'the supreme arbitrament of arms' – in the characteristic phrase of Edward Carson (1854–1935) – was about to be answered when the declaration of war on 4 August 1914 postponed, with Redmond's agreement, any decision about Home Rule. His policy of 'good behaviour', as opposed to Ulster intransigence, was continually betrayed by Britain, and his encouragement of recruiting which would, he believed, leave him after a short war with a trained army that could enforce the terms of the Home Rule legislation meant that many Irishmen, including his brother, died in the trenches of the First World War.

There were other elements in the political situation that were to be highly significant. On 1 November 1913, Professor Eoin MacNeill, one of the founders of the Gaelic League, had responded to the UVF gun-running by writing an article in the League's journal *An Claidheamh Soluis* called 'The North Began' which recommended that the Home Rulers, like the UVF, should arm themselves. He was responsible for the founding of the Irish Volunteers three weeks later. Already, too, the rekindled phoenix flame fanned by John Devoy (1842–1928), the head of the American Fenian offshoot, Clan na Gael, had burst into a small but steady fire and as the regenerated Irish Republican Brotherhood (IRB) had become the incandescent element of the Volunteers. The third important force which had been generated by the Dublin lockout of 1913 was the Citizen Army of the labour leader James Connolly (1868–1916).

The 1916 Rising, in which members of these groups took part, was at first greeted by rage and derision but the dignity of the participants and the deliberately paced executions of its leaders by General Maxwell (1859–1929) resulted in a wave of support for Arthur Griffith's Sinn Féin. Many of the Volunteers, released from prison as a result of a mitigation of Maxwell's absolutism and the pressure of world opinion, constituted themselves as the Irish Republican Army (IRA) – an indication of their aim – and their numbers were swollen by young volunteers and returned, seasoned soldiers. Though nominally under the control of Sinn Féin, the various IRA forces had a great deal of local autonomy and one of the reasons for the drift into hostilities against the British was the lack of central control. The first shots of the War of Independence, in the ambush by Dan Breen and Seán Treacy (1895–1920) at Soloheadbeg, County Tipperary, on 21 January 1919, was such a local (and not formally unauthorised) operation.

The spirit of the times held life cheap; 10 million had died in the First World War and the quasi-religious fervour of 1916 still fired the more extreme republicans, notably Michael Collins, who was an effective general of operations. Many young men, imbued with exalted patriotism and having a role to play for the first time in their mundane lives, welcomed the call to arms. Pure, self-regarding republicanism, in which no sacrifice of self or others was too great for the cause, was by definition tunnel-visioned, and it left the participants with no urge to negotiate and ill-equipped to do so should the need arise. De Valera, who had feared and loathed violence since his days as a successful Easter Week commander, knew that a war was almost inevitable in the circumstances but did his best to avert it, knowing that some kind of negotiated settlement was inevitable. The attitude of the British government – the coalition that was led by Lloyd George from 1916 but was heavily dependent on the support of the extreme unionist, the Canadian Bonar Law – was notably unhelpful. The arrest of de Valera and Griffith in May 1918 on the fictitious charge that they were involved in a German plot left Collins and Cathal Brugha free to prepare for a chosen armed confrontation.

One less-noticed result of the Rising was that Lloyd George decided in June 1916 to partition the country, giving Home Rule to most of Ireland but excluding the 'Protestant' north-east. Redmond did what he could to fight the proposal and succeeded in cutting the counties of exclusion from the nine counties of historical Ulster to the six that presently constitute Northern Ireland, while accepting Lloyd George's assurance that the exclusion would be temporary. When in 1920 the IRA were engaged in their war essentially against the Home Rule proposals originally agreed by Redmond, Lloyd George passed, virtually without opposition, the Government of Ireland Act, which set up regimes in Dublin and Belfast. Sinn Féin's policy of abstention meant that there was no parliamentary debate and no possibility of mitigation of the measure, which left the Ulster nationalists (a third of the population) permanently under unionist governments which were to last until 18 July 1973, when the Belfast parliament was abolished. Just as during the Treaty negotiations, minds were concentrated on other topics.

The invitation to treat was to expose in the republican side considerable divisions, which had been ignored during the fighting. The delegation had against them the Welsh wizard Lloyd George, the most consummate and capable politician of the age, and he was backed by Churchill, the most charismatic leader of the next generation. The negotiations, over which hung the threat of a British ultimatum (finally pronounced by Lloyd George as 'war within three days' on 6 December 1921), were long and tortuous in the extreme; Lord Longford's magisterial book on the subject, *Peace by Ordeal* (1935), was well named. There were two unexpected features of the team of delegates: the presence of Michael Collins and the absence of de Valera. Collins probably accepted his role out of duty, although his name was as strongly associated with hardline militarism as were those of Cathal Brugha (who refused to go to London), Austin Stack, Oscar Traynor and Rory O'Connor (who did not even approve the truce). His presence there was intended as an assurance that any agreement by him would be accepted by the IRA.

De Valera's motives for remaining in Dublin are still uncertain. Critics say that he resented the growth of Collins' personal standing, which had surprised him on his return from his fund-raising tour of the United States (1 June 1919–23 December 1920). They say, too, that he knew from earlier discussions with Lloyd George that the likely outcome of the negotiations would be a compromise unacceptable to many republicans and he did not wish to be associated with that 'betrayal'. This view is almost certainly unjust and too simplistic, considering the subtle, not to say machiavellian, nature of the president's mind. (It also ignores the sense of moral scruple that he believed permeated his whole existence.) He was busy working on an 'external association' arrangement that was eventually called Document No. 2 and which he thought would have been more palatable to the ultras in the vexed question of the remaining connection with Britain and the oath of allegiance. He was regarded (and regarded himself) as a kind of head of state and as such should not, he felt, be engaged in the minutiae of negotiation any more than George V. He hoped, too, that in the event of open and armed hostility to Treaty terms, he would have a sufficiently impartial air to prevent extreme violence.

The team were regarded (certainly by the British) as 'plenipotentiaries' who had the power to make final decisions, but this was later disputed. The important question of Ulster, which should have been the clause on which negotiations broke down, went by default; as before, in the debate on the Government of Ireland Act, the southern nationalists allowed themselves to be distracted. They settled for Lloyd George's offer of a boundary commission, which they believed would deliver counties Tyrone and Fermanagh, Derry city and Newry into the new Free State. They knew that this would still leave many nationalists under a government which would regard them with suspicion and which would use most of its energies to prevent them having access to political power, but they could not take seriously the idea that Northern Ireland might have other than a very temporary existence. Collins was already considering a policy of non-cooperation with the new state; he intended this policy to become more aggressive as time went on.

In fact the fate of the north was not of immediate concern to the more vociferous republican anti-Treatyites; what they wanted was a republic and a complete break with the king and commonwealth. The document that Griffith and Collins signed limited Irish independence in several ways: the Irish Free State would have the same status within the empire as Canada; there would be a governor-general, the king's representative; the royal navy and the RAF would have rights of operation in certain Irish ports; and the members of the Dáil would have to swear allegiance (in the first instance) to the constitution of the Irish Free State and then to the king and his successors 'in virtue of the common citizenship of Ireland with

Great Britain' and her membership of the British Commonwealth of Nations. The order of swearing was regarded
as significant but in the end did not signify; those who
accepted the terms shrugged their shoulders and followed
the form; nothing on earth would have moved the ultras
even to recognise the 'crown' let alone swear allegiance to
it. The irrelevant crown had the same iconic power for the
British as the idea of a free, independent Irish republic had
for the IRA, but its imposition as a condition on republicans was notably unhelpful in the circumstances.

Document No. 2, de Valera's alternative, would have
placed all authority with the Irish people but would have
bound them in an association with other members of the
existing commonwealth, recognising the king as president of the association. Significantly, there was no oath
of greater allegiance than befitted the recognition of the
king as head of the commonwealth. Of equal importance
was the temporary acquiescence in the Treaty terms with
regard to Northern Ireland. De Valera had hoped that this
compromise would satisfy the more extreme republicans
but they would not – and psychologically could not – settle
for anything less than a free republic. It was what Pearse
had died for, and the spirit of Easter Week was still alive.
In the circumstances, ingenious as Document No. 2 was,
it was not acceptable to the British side either. Indeed the
terms of the Treaty as accepted by the plenipotentiaries

appalled the Conservatives, Bonar Law claiming that these terms left Sinn Féin the option of in time declaring the republic that it sought. In this he unwittingly anticipated Collins' description of the agreement in Dáil Éireann on 19 December, thirteen days after the signing, as 'the freedom to obtain freedom'.

13

THE FOUR COURTS

The Treaty terms were vigorously debated in the Dáil on twelve days between 14 December and 7 January – the Christmas recess lasting from 22 December until 3 January. The debates took place in the council chamber of UCD in Earlsfort Terrace because the Mansion House in Dawson Street, where the first Dáil had met, was occupied by a Christmas fête. Many of the TDs were IRA commanders who had been returned unopposed in the 1920 election. Though the candidates had a considerable following there was undoubtedly a certain amount of local intimidation. The 1918 Dáil had been elected on a minority vote and there is some justice in the assertion that the personalities who were now settling Ireland's future were just about representative of the country's wishes. On Thursday 15 December de Valera proposed his own document, withdrawing it again on the nineteenth when Griffith introduced the motion, seconded by Seán MacEoin, 'that Dáil Éireann approves the Treaty between Great Britain and Ireland signed in London on December 6th, 1921'. He had discovered by then that the population at large was strongly in favour of the terms. A majority of the plain people of Ireland were anxious to accept what seemed to them very good terms, unaware that they agreed instinctively with Collins when he wrote in a letter to a friend on the day the Treaty was signed: 'Think – what I have got for Ireland! Something which she has wanted these past seven hundred years.' (The letter continued with ominous accuracy: 'Will anyone be satisfied at the bargain? Will anyone? I tell you this – early this morning I signed my death warrant.')

De Valera's incessant but carefully modulated contributions were in noted contrast to the exalted and fiery speeches of the other anti-Treaty members. Only once during the nightmarish drift towards civil war did he engage in apocalyptic republican rhetoric: on St Patrick's Day at Thurles in an almost hysterical speech he spoke of the need the IRA might have to 'wade through Irish blood, through the blood of the soldiers of the Irish government and through, perhaps, the blood of some of the members of the government in order to get Irish freedom'. Supporters say the speech was meant as a warning; critics, with more justice, condemn it as incitement; as prophecy it proved to be only too precise.

Most of the anti-Treatyites spoke of betrayal – the more extreme members unmoved by the pragmatic logic of Griffith and rejecting Collins' interpretation of the agreement's potential. They had elevated the cause of Ireland's republican freedom to the level almost of religious belief. No mere considerations of the possible were to be allowed to leaven the purity of the ideals of the 1916 Proclamation. The exaltation of battle was no preparation for the fustian business of democracy and in the heat of the verbal rancour the opposition did not seem to realise that the Treatyites shared their sense of disappointment. Most had no concept of the tedium of much parliamentary business and, as the reports of proceedings show, parliamentary language had not been learned. Old comrades found themselves on opposing sides and personal animosities that had been papered over during the war now showed as gaping cracks. Cathal Brugha in a characteristically intemperate outburst decried Collins' contribution to the success of the struggle, claiming that he was a mere publicity-seeker, a creation of the newspapers. Erskine Childers, who had acted as secretary to the delegation but had not signed the Treaty, revealed himself as one of the agreement's coldest and most bitter opponents. He was joined in extreme rhetoric by the women of the Dáil, including Pearse's mother, Terence MacSwiney's sister, Tom Clarke's widow and the Countess Markievicz – which caused the group to be known, with the inevitable splash of black Irish humour, as the 'women and Childers party'.

The Dáil approved the Treaty on 7 January 1922 but by
a very close margin: sixty-four to fifty-seven. Two days later
de Valera resigned the presidency of the Dáil and when
on 10 January he was rejected on a motion of re-election
by sixty votes to fifty-eight he walked out of the room,
followed by the rest of the 'antis'. Tempers were high:
Collins shouted 'Deserters all!' to be answered by cries
of 'Up the Republic!' and when Constance Markievicz
called the remaining deputies oath-breakers and cowards,
Collins roared 'Foreigners! Americans! English!' – a not-
too-subtle reference to the presumed nationalities of the
countess, de Valera and Childers. It was clear that most of
the IRA commanders – such as Rory O'Connor, director
of engineering during the war; Cathal Brugha, IRA chief
of staff; Austin Stack, deputy chief of staff; Liam Mellows;
Liam Lynch; and Ernie O'Malley – and many others would
accept neither the terms of the Treaty nor the nature
and personnel of the Provisional Government that was
about to be set up as the British authorities began the
handover of power. Personal psychology was as significant
a determinant of decision as record of active service and
idealism. There were no more grimly dedicated activists
in the war than Collins, Richard Mulcahy and Seán Mac-
Eoin; yet they were prepared to accept the terms and work
within them eventually to improve them. Another factor,
impossible fully to interpret, was the fact that most of the

dramatis personae were under forty. Only Arthur Griffith, who was to die the following August at the age of fifty-one, was the more likely age for a statesman.

The fissure grew wider, causing a sociological and psychological split in the country and providing a hateful means of personal identification for nearly three generations of Irish people who should have been looking eagerly forwards rather than meanly backwards. Even now the rancour of the time can surface in unlikely and petty controversies. The response of the 'antis' was instinctively militaristic. Power, in the shape of arms, rested with the largely anti-Treaty IRA. Collins and Mulcahy worked as swiftly as they could to build up a legitimate national force that would be the arm of the Provisional Government that slowly edged out of the Dáil. Rory O'Connor, who had emerged as the chief spokesman for those who were soon to be called the 'Irregulars', demanded a convention of what Mulcahy still referred to as the 'army of the Republic'. The latter temporised, finding excellent reasons for postponing what promised to be an incendiary gathering.

Meanwhile the handover of power was going more smoothly than anyone had expected. A significant moment was the 'surrender' of Dublin Castle to Collins by Lord Fitzalan, the viceroy. One probably true anecdote from the event states that he chided Collins for being seven minutes late and Collins replied, 'We've been waiting seven hundred years; you can have the seven minutes.' The British army's strength was steadily diminished until by May 1922 only the Dublin garrison of 5,000 men remained, and by the time the demobilisation of the RIC began, at the end of March, all the Black and Tans and Auxiliaries had gone away to cover themselves with further glory. Not all approved of the ending of the army connection; in garrison towns like Athlone and Fermoy the soldiers' commissariat contracts and individual buying power were sorely missed. And the departure of the RIC, on the whole a respected force, left the country effectively without any formal system of maintenance of public order outside Dublin, where the lofty members of the Dublin Metropolitan Police still patrolled the streets.

This hiatus began to be filled on 21 February with the establishment of the civic guard, whose members at the start of their careers had side arms but no uniforms. The force was intended to replicate the RIC but unrest among the members led to a mutiny in August. Eoin O'Duffy, who had been assistant chief of staff of the IRA, working under instruction from Kevin O'Higgins, was given the task of reconstruction, and the body he produced, the garda síochána, an unarmed consensual force established on 8 August 1923, quickly gained public support. The civic guard figured in the ultimatum issued by the anti-Treatyites under O'Connor and Mellows after they occupied the Four Courts and other city centre buildings on 13 April. They wanted its disbandment and refused to recognise the Provisional Government, which was determined to maintain the army as the IRA. They would not countenance the holding of any election 'while the threat of war by England exists'.

The choice of the Four Courts (and the buildings on the east side of O'Connell Street) was symbolic rather than tactical, much as that of the GPO had been exactly six years earlier. As ever, symbols took precedence over practicalities; the destruction of the Law Library and the Public Record Office, with priceless archive records of a thousand years of Irish history, was motivated by the same nihilism. Flickering flames of anti-Treatyite activity had already been noted around the country, and Mulcahy's armed forces did what they could do quench them. Anti-Treatyites had some successful seizures of arms at Helvic Head in Waterford and Cobh harbour. The occupation of Beggars Bush barracks on 1 February by pro-Treaty forces (sent in at 4 a.m.) prevented the anti-Treatyites from seizing it, and an internal coup planned for the eve of the Volunteer Convention of 26 March was forestalled. The Civil War, as a whole, was fought by forces not entirely loyal on either side. Many of the prison guards in Mountjoy were sympathetic to the anti-Treatyite prisoners and there was no operational split in the IRA in the north, since both

factions were active in doing what they could to defend
Northern Ireland Catholics against essentially govern-
ment-approved pogroms. Collins and Mulcahy found
themselves in the anomalous position of supplying arms to
anti-Treatyites in Belfast and Derry. The situation there,
though forecast precisely by northern nationalists, seemed,
as did most things in Northern Ireland, to surprise Dublin.
One of the direr aspects of the internecine struggle in the
south was that it distracted Collins' attention from the
crisis in Northern Ireland.

The first indication of a serious threat of civil war was
the Army Convention, held in in the Mansion House on
26 March 1922, in spite of the fact that it had been prohibited by Mulcahy. The 220 anti-Treaty delegates from
forty-nine brigades were still smarting from the occupation
of Limerick by pro-Treaty forces – urban fighting was prevented only by the personal intervention of Oscar Traynor
and Liam Lynch. After the convention its spokesman
Rory O'Connor repudiated the authority of Dáil Éireann,
clearly expecting that any election would reaffirm com-
mitment to the Treaty terms. O'Connor was asked if he
agreed that the logical inference of his ultimatum was
a military dictatorship; his reply was typical of the man
and the movement: 'You can take it that way if you like.'
(In time O'Connor would repudiate even the anti-Treaty
council, when they refused him permission to attack the

remaining British forces in Ireland.) The first victims of
the now openly militant anti-Treatyites were the presses of
the pro-Treaty *Freeman's Journal* (1763–1924), which had
not reported the convention to their satisfaction.

Still anxious to prevent greater hostilities, Collins and
de Valera worked during May on a pact that would essentially rig the results of the general election that was due
to create the third Dáil. (De Valera did not necessarily
believe in democratic principles at the time: he was at his
most pedagogical – or even episcopal – when he stated
that 'the majority have not the right to do wrong'. His remarkable conscience was able to ignore the statement by
the Catholic hierarchy on 26 April that they considered
that 'the best and wisest course is for Ireland to accept the
Treaty and make the most of the freedom that it undoubtedly brings'.) By the terms of the pact all nationalist
candidates would stand as Sinn Féin, unopposed and in
proportion to the seats they held in the second Dáil. The
pact caused uproar in Westminster and resulted in the
same kind of anti-Catholic activity in the north that had
followed the occupation of the Four Courts. The Treaty
visibly trembled, with threats from London of closing the
border and of occupying Dublin. Collins and Griffith
again yielded to the threat of a new British onslaught. In
the election which followed on 16 June the anti-Treatyites
were decisively defeated and the results showed the begin-

nings of more normal politics: Pro-Treaty, 58; Anti-Treaty 36; Labour, 17; Farmers, 7; Independents, 6; TCD, 6.

Before the full significance of these results could be analysed the assassination of Field Marshal Sir Henry Wilson on 22 June by two IRA members, Reginald Dunne and Joseph O'Sullivan, who were hanged on 10 August, caused a further crisis. Wilson had figured largely in the Curragh incident and as security adviser to the Northern Ireland government was held responsible for the Norther Ireland pogroms. (The day after his death three Catholic youths were shot in cold blood by B-specials in Cushendall, County Antrim.) It is likely that Collins knew and approved of the killing. It precipitated the formal opening of the war, which is dated from the pro-Treaty attack on the Four Courts at 4 a.m. on 28 June. Lloyd George had written immediately to Collins, demanding that he take action against the Dublin anti-Treatyites, assuming – or choosing to assume – that it had been an anti-Treatyite operation. General Macready, the Dublin GOC, was ordered to take the courts on 24 June but wisely ignored his instructions, knowing that it would spell the end of the Treaty. As it was he provided Collins with the artillery which finally brought about the surrender. Collins still hesitated but the kidnapping of General J. J. ('Ginger') O'Connell in reprisal for the arrest of Leo Henderson, who had tried to commandeer cars to mount an attack on the north, caused him to give the order to evacuate the Four Courts and surrender the garrison.

The defenders issued a characteristic communiqué which called upon 'our former comrades of the Irish Republic to return to that allegiance and thus guard the Nation's honour from the infamous stigma that her sons aided her foes in retaining a hateful domination over her.' It also apostrophied 'the sacred spirits of the illustrious Dead' who were with them 'in this great struggle'. The taking of a 'British' institution with British shells turned on fellow Irishmen gave them another symbolic victory but it was clear that the now well-armed pro-Treaty forces, who had the option of using British soldiers, would be the inevitable victors. Though outnumbered 'down the country' in the ratio 4:1, they soon secured Dublin. The city conflict left 65 dead and 281 seriously wounded, the most notable casualty being Cathal Brugha, who rushed out into Talbot Street from the back of his headquarters in the Granville Hotel, shooting at the lines of pro-Treaty troops. He died two days later. The members of the Four Courts garrison, including O'Connor and Mellows, were interned in Mountjoy. On 8 August Cork was taken by sea and by the end of that month, one of the most tragic in Ireland's history, the Civil War had become a grisly copy of the opportunistic raid-and-ambush pattern of the Anglo-Irish War.

14

EMERGENCY POWERS

Worried by continuing violence in Northern Ireland – in which nationalist dead and severely wounded were in the ratio of 4:1 to Protestant fatalities and which tended to break out in response to events in the south – and weary of the grind of politics, Collins turned with something like relief and even his old enthusiasm to the task of finishing the war as quickly as possible. The horror of it appalled him and he resented the emotional toll of the idea of a brothers' conflict. He was ever-anxious to find some kind of peaceful settlement but was determined to end hostilities by force if necessary. At the start of the fighting the anti-Treatyites had a majority of trained men and arms but this disproportion was dealt with by intensive recruiting into the national army and a steady supply of guns and ammunition, including field artillery, from Britain. By the end of the war Britain had provided £1 million worth of arms and supplies to the Free State.

On 20 July both Waterford and Limerick were secured by government forces, the latter after vicious fighting at Kil-

mallock, and the IRA, now led by Liam Lynch, fell behind
a line between those cities that could mark a notional eastern boundary of his 'Munster Republic'. Lynch had been
captured during the fighting in Dublin but was released by
Mulcahy in the belief that as an internal adversary of Rory
O'Connor he would act as a kind of demobiliser. In fact
he became an implacable pursuer of the fighting, growing
more resolute with each reverse. His forces reverted to the
guerrilla tactics that they had perfected during the Anglo-
Irish War, but now with nothing like the support they had
enjoyed then. Even then some of the 'support' resulted not
from approval of the cause but out of intimidation; now
Treatyites could expect little quarter. Kevin O'Higgins,
one of the younger (born 1892) but most effective members of the cabinet described the anti-Treatyites' activities
as consisting of 20 per cent idealism, 20 per cent crime
and 60 per cent 'sheer futility'. The pattern of robbing
banks and post offices, blowing up bridges and unofficial
billeting that was characteristic of the earlier struggle
seemed to most of the population – even of Munster —to
be pointless. Battles at Dundalk, Blessington, Clonmel,
Sligo, Tuam, Tipperary and Cahir were followed by the
withdrawal of anti-Treaty forces.

One of Collins' closest friends, Harry Boland, was shot
by a young soldier during an arrest attempt at a hotel in
Skerries on 31 July. Accounts of the incident range from

the view that the incident constituted the shooting down of an unarmed man to the idea that it was a killing to prevent the escape of a known anti-Treatyites quartermaster. What actually happened is unclear but Boland had demanded to see the officer in charge and was moving towards the door of his bedroom when the shot that caused his death three days later was fired. Collins grieved even more at the death of his closest friend than over that of his old comrade Brugha. The terrible pain of a civil war in a small country, fought between old comrades, was becoming very clear. Collins, now commander in chief, was ever more anxious to end the killing and used all his capacity for undercover initiative to try to arrange to talk to Lynch and the other members of the anti-Treatyites who were still holding out.

Fermoy, the last town held by them, was evacuated on 11 August but any satisfaction the government might have felt was dissipated by the sudden death of Griffith from a cerebral haemorrhage the next morning. He had been ill for some weeks (and was clearly weary of the bitterness and attrition that the Treaty had engendered) but insisted in carrying on cabinet business. In a sense his work was done; his foundation of Sinn Féin and insistence on the Irishness of Ireland had made a huge contribution to the national confidence and laid the intellectual and social basis for an independent country. His mien during the eight months of his presidency was appropriate for the time, consolidating the new state in spite of violent opposition to its survival and holding out for democracy against the more convenient militarism.

Collins' decision to go to Cork after Griffith's funeral was disapproved of by many of his closest advisers. He would be travelling through anti-Treatyite country and, whatever boost to morale his physical presence might engender, the risks seemed too great. His main purpose was the hope of negotiating an end to the killing, and it seemed incumbent upon him to go into 'enemy' territory, since the anti-Treatyites were in no position – and had little inclination – to come to him. Though in poor physical and mental shape and deeply depressed by the condition of the country, north and south, he insisted with forced cheerfulness that ' ... my fellow countrymen won't kill me'. Anti-Treatyite intelligence, however, knew he was going to be in his native county and the prize was irresistible. An ambush party was in position at Béal na mBláth on the Bandon–Macroom road for most of the day of Tuesday 22 August and was on the point of breaking up when Collins' party arrived. It is generally agreed that if, as he was advised, the small convoy had driven fast along the road – blockaded only by a cart, which was quickly removed – Collins would have been safe. Instead he seized a rifle and returned fire. He was hit by a ricochet in the base of the skull and was dead by 9.30 that August evening.

The blow to the country was incalculable: Northern Ireland nationalists had lost the one member of the Dublin government who had kept their plight perpetually before his eyes and who might have had the charisma and intelligence to secure better conditions from the unionist government; the anti-Treatyites no longer had a friend at court – one who knew and understood the depth of their feelings and who might have prevented the atrocities on both sides that were the rule in the latter days of the struggle; the government, already bereft of Griffith's political experience and moral force, lost a vigorous, intelligent and maturing statesman; and the country lost its 'laughing boy', its folk hero, whose handsome physical presence, emphasised in his general's uniform, might in the end have won the ideal of a united, independent, peaceful Ireland. De Valera had known that Collins was in Cork and was aware of the intention to ambush him. He dreaded it for the typical reason that '... he was a big man and might negotiate. If things fall into the hands of lesser men there is no telling what might happen.' He tried without success to get the local brigade to call off the ambush and after Collins' death did what he could to persuade Lynch to stop the war, with equal lack of success.

Collins' funeral in Glasnevin on 28 August attracted huge crowds but the story of his official reputation since is a miserable one. While de Valera was in power or in a position of influence he did what he could to play down Collins' reputation and significance. Successive Fianna Fáil governments did everything in their power to hinder the Collins family from erecting a suitable memorial over what was a simple military grave. De Valera personally withheld permission for a cross of Carrara marble and insisted upon a limestone one, the total cost not to exceed £300 and the erection to be private and with no publicity. As late as 1965 a handbook entitled *Facts about Ireland*, published by the department of foreign affairs, had no photograph of Collins and the following year de Valera refused to become a patron of a Michael Collins Foundation, set up by the subject's old friend Joe McGrath (1887–1966), the founder of the Irish Hospitals Trust. Insofar as history is understood or even known by later generations, Collins' name lives on as that of a hero of Irish history and is now even better known than Pearse, Parnell or O'Connell, thanks to the success of Neil Jordan's almost historical film about him. Its making was perhaps timely; the Irish are not obsessed by their history, as their detractors claim, but rather are held in the vice of imprecise prejudice.

Though many of Collins' old comrades on the anti-Treaty side were devastated by the unthinkable loss that his death represented, their more immediate concern was fear of reprisal. The numbers of those guarding anti-

Treatyite prisoners had to be increased to prevent private punitive response. Mulcahy, a vigorous if less gifted man than Collins, did what he could to continue the dead general's military policies, insofar as he could interpret them. The cabinet had decided even before the third Dáil met on 9 September to appoint William Cosgrave, who had been acting chairman since Griffith's death, as president. He proved a conservative and stoical politician – a safe pair of hands who would patiently create the new Free State out of its revolutionary disarray, give it its honourable if unadventurous character and prepare it for its maturity as a nation state. The choice was deliberate since, although he had fought in 1916 (with Eamon Ceannt and Cathal Brugha in the South Dublin Union), he was a civilian and left the continuation of the war to Mulcahy, who was appointed GOC of the Provisional Government's armed forces. The separation of the two systems was deliberate, a counter to any suggestion of a military dictatorship and a deliberate contrast to the perceived intentions of O'Connor and Lynch.

The autumn of 1922 saw the beginnings of the guerrilla war west of the Shannon and south of the Suir. Connacht had been relatively quiet during the Anglo-Irish War and it was not always possible to determine whether the Civil War incidents there were part of the current struggle or a recrudescence of much older hatreds. There was some activity around Tuam in July, August and September but in general things were low-key. The province had its share of the frightfulness of reprisal execution as the bitterness of the conflict intensified during the winter and the following spring. Between 28 September and 10 October an order, largely the work of Kevin O'Higgins, was rushed through the Dáil; the order announced an amnesty for all who were willing to lay down their arms 'in the present state of armed rebellion and insurrection' but gave the Army Council special powers to try in military courts and punish anyone who was in breach of the regulations, which became law on 15 October.

The offences – which could be punished by, in ascending order, fine, internment, imprisonment, deportation, penal servitude and death – included the 'taking part in or aiding and abetting any attacks upon the National forces'; looting, arson and other damage to public or private property; and, most significantly, the possession of 'any bomb, or articles in the nature of a bomb, or any dynamite, or gelignite, or other explosive substance, or any revolver, rifle, gun or other firearm or lethal weapon, or any ammunition for such firearm'. The document was issued from general headquarters, Portobello Barracks, on 10 October and signed on behalf of the Army Council by Risteárd Ua Maolcatha, general commander in chief. At about the same time, in what was regarded as a form of interference with the freedom of the press, special instructions were sent from government offices to editors and subs as to nomenclature in relation to the reporting of incidents in the war. The army was to be referred to as the 'national army', 'Irish army' or just 'troops'; the anti-Treatyites were not to be described as either 'forces' or 'troops', nor were their leaders to be given their ranks; articles or letters about the treatment of anti-Treatyite prisoners were not to be published and in newspaper stories the words 'republicans', 'attacked', 'commandeered' and 'arrested' were to be replaced by 'Irregulars', 'fired at', 'seized' and 'kidnapped' respectively. Something very like the martial law that Rory O'Connor had threatened had been imposed by the Treatyites.

A document that came from a different source but was just as compelling for some of the concerned parties was read at all masses on Sunday 22 October. The Irish Catholic hierarchy, which had already indicated its attitude to the Treaty by its statement in April, now published a joint pastoral condemning anti-Treatyite resistance to the Provisional Government and its forces. The letter, signed by Cardinal Logue (1840–1924) and the other bishops, said that 'a section of the community' had 'wrecked Ireland from end to end', that 'a Republic without popular recognition behind it is a contradiction in terms' and that 'all those ... who participate in such crimes are guilty of the gravest sins and may not be absolved in Confession, nor admitted to Holy Communion, if they purpose to persevere in such evil courses'. Apologists for the anti-Treaty forces have regarded this excommunication as the granting of a kind of licence to the Provisional Government to proceed with seventy-seven executions of anti-Treatyite prisoners between November and the following May. This view is rather simplistic and the reasoning behind it flawed but the church's stance did increase the government's moral authority in its extreme response to anti-Treatyite attacks. From the perspective of seventy-five years the executions strike us as draconian, but they were perceived as necessary at the time and there were few complaints about them from the population at large.

The first well-known figure to die was Erskine Childers, who had been execrated as an 'Englishman' by the pro-Treatyites and had been an extremely effective chief of anti-Treatyite propaganda. He was arrested on 11 November and found to be in possession of a gun – a pearl-handled revolver that had been a present from Collins. This was a technicality but it was enough to secure the death penalty for four 'unknowns' – James Fisher, Peter Cassidy, John F. Gaffney and Richard Twohig – who were executed six days later in Kilmainham. As it was, Childers was shot (on 14 November) while awaiting the result of an appeal – a flagrant breach of his civil rights. The grief and vengeful rage at Collins' killing were still strong. These deaths were followed on 30 November by an order from Liam Lynch that all TDs who had voted for the legislation under which Childers had been executed were to be shot on sight. A week later, on 7 December, Seán Hales and the leas-ceann comhairle of the Dáil, Pádraic Ó Máille, were attacked while travelling to the Dáil in an open car. Hales died and Ó Máille was seriously wounded.

The cabinet met and selected from the anti-Treatyite prisoners four representatives of the movement – Rory O'Connor (who had been Kevin O'Higgins' best man), Liam Mellows, Joe McKelvey and Richard Barrett – one from each province; they were executed the next morning in Mountjoy. This course of action was ruthless but effective since no further attacks were made on TDs but the wound inflicted by that decision festered for years and was the main cause of the death of O'Higgins' father, who was shot in his home in Stradbally, Queen's County (Laois), on 11 February 1923, and of his own death four and a half years later. On 10 December the house of Seán McGarry, TD, was fired while one of his children was still inside and it was said that rescue attempts were forbidden. The boy died and the verdict of the inquest was wilful murder. It was as bleak a Christmas as Ireland had experienced for many years.

In spite of the tales of killings, torture of prisoners and

general frightfulness the political machine continued to operate. The Irish Free State (officially 'Saorstát Éireann') came into existence on 6 December 1922 and its first postage stamp, value 2d, showing a map of Ireland, was issued. (For other denominations British stamps, with the head of George V overprinted with 'Saorstát Éireann', continued to be used.) Tim Healy, Parnell's nemesis, was appointed governor-general-designate by George V. The Senate had its first meeting on 11 December, with Lord Glenavy (1851–1931), father of the humorist Patrick Campbell, as its chairman. It was clear that the Free State was a fact; it was becoming clearer that the Northern Ireland state, then relatively peaceful, was also a fact. Anti-Treatyism was beaten but the mopping-up would be protracted and bloody. The mindset of the anti-Treatyites, if anything, hardened, and 'military necessity', to use Mulcahy's phrase, was used on both sides to excuse murderous brutality. Yeats' 'terrible beauty' had become a terrible ugliness.

15

LEGION OF THE REARGUARD

The 'tide of bitterness', to use de Valera's words written in an article in the American journal the *Irish Word*, continued to rise. On 8 January 1923 eight Free State soldiers were executed for treachery and there were fears of mutiny and largescale desertions. On the same day the Army Council issued another stark order extending the power of the military courts and in a fuller statement on 1 February assumed the option of executing any person having possession of any 'plan, document or note, for a purpose prejudicial to the safety of the State or of the National forces'.

Throughout the conflict the implacability of the leaders was mitigated somewhat by the wavering of absolute allegiance on both sides but local confrontations could result in such atrocities as to suggest that scores from much older times were being settled. Seventeen anti-Treatyite prisoners were killed in the first fortnight of March in County Kerry alone. In one particularly nauseating incident at Ballyseedy on 7 March, in reprisal for the dynamiting at Knocknagoshel of five 'Staters' (one of whom had a reputation for torturing prisoners), eight men were tied to a log and blown to pieces by a mine, a ninth miraculously escaping when he was blown clear. In Cahirciveen on 12 March the same technique was used on five others, with the added refinement that they were shot in the legs first. Donegal, too, had its own incident when on 14 March four IRA men – Charlie Daly, Tim O'Sullivan, Dan Enright and Seán Larkin – were executed at Drumboe, in woods near Stranorlar. There were no unsavoury details of these killings apart from the summary nature of the executions – the automatic sentence for those found carrying arms.

Efforts to end the killings continued; Liam Deasy, who had led an IRA brigade in west Cork, was by now convinced that the prolongation of the war was pointless and actually damaging to the republican cause. He was about to make his feelings known to the anti-Treatyite executive when in mid-January he was captured by Free State soldiers and sentenced to death. While being held in Clonmel Borstal he decided to approach his captors with a plan to appeal to other commanders to surrender. Later in Arbour Hill he agreed to sign a document worded by the Free State authorities:

> I have undertaken for the future of Ireland to accept and aid in the immediate and unconditional surrender of all arms and men as required by General Mulcahy.

This declaration having been signed, he was permitted to elaborate his reasons in a longer document. It had an inevitable effect on morale and in its common sense appealed to all but the most adamant of the IRA leaders. Lynch was not convinced and called a meeting of sixteen senior commandants on 24 March in the remote Nire Valley in County Waterford. De Valera attended (although he was not allowed to take part in the significant deliberations), bringing proposals which amounted to an acceptance of the Treaty terms but with freedom granted to objectors to pursue the ultimate ideal of an independent republican state by non-violent means. Lynch could not be persuaded that the battle, if not the war, had been lost and was able to persuade others to join with him in defeating the peace proposals by six votes to five.

The war dragged on as cruelties on both sides continued. It was clear by the end of spring that the Free State forces were massing for a final solution. Then on 10 April Liam Lynch was mortally wounded in an engagement near Newcastle in his stronghold in the Knockmealdowns. Frank Aiken, who replaced him as chief of staff and who had spoken fervently for the acceptance of de Valera's proposals the previous month, was anxious now for their acceptance. He declared a unilateral ceasefire on 30 April. Cosgrave rejected any peace proposals which did not include decommissioning of arms held by the IRA and he

could not by the accepted constitution permit republican
TDs who had not taken the oath of allegiance to sit in the
Dáil. Any continuation of the struggle was now accepted
as murderous folly; on 24 May Aiken ordered anti-Treaty
troops still in the field to 'dump arms'. The call to give
up the struggle was accompanied by a message addressed
rather operatically to the 'Soldiers of the Republic, Legion
of the Rearguard' by de Valera. It began:

> The Republic can no longer be defended successfully by
> your arms. Further sacrifice of life would now be vain and
> continuance of the struggle in arms unwise in the national
> interest and prejudicial to the future of our cause. Military
> victory must be allowed to rest with those who have des-
> troyed the Republic. Other means must be sought to safe-
> guard the nation's right.

He went on to reassure them that 'much that you set out
to accomplish is achieved' and that the people, exhausted
by seven years of intense effort, would 'rally again to the
standard' and that 'when they are ready, you will be, and
your place will be again as of old with the vanguard'.

As well as the seventy-seven republicans who had been
executed (including six in Tuam, three in Tralee and three
in Ennis as late as April and May 1923), there were 850
other casualties. The numbers imprisoned or interned had
reached a total of 11,480 by 1 July; these included all the
surviving anti-Treatyite commanders, among them Austin
Stack and Dan Breen, who were captured on 14 and 17

April respectively, and Seán Lemass, who was later to be responsible for the modernisation of the Irish economy. De Valera was arrested while electioneering in Ennis on 15 August, was kept in solitary confinement for six months and was not released until 16 July 1924. On 14 October 424 prisoners held in Mountjoy went on hunger strike and those held in Kilmainham and other prisons and internment camps joined them. The strike had lasted until 23 November 1923, with two hunger strikers dying – Captain Denis Barry on 20 November in Newbridge Camp and Captain Andrew Sullivan in Mountjoy on 22 November.

Most of the internees, not having been convicted of any crime, were freed in the summer of 1924, and a general amnesty was declared on 8 November. One year later the Boundary Commission, which all the Treaty delegates and de Valera believed would allow nationalist areas to opt out of the new state of Northern Ireland and help make it ungovernable, proved to be an empty formula. Sir James Craig had declared on 7 October 1925 that if its findings were unacceptable to the Northern Ireland parliament he would resign to lead the defence of any territory 'unfairly transferred'. On 7 November the right-wing *Morning Post* 'leaked' the news that the commission would make no substantial changes, and O'Higgins went to Westminster on the twenty-fourth to prepare the tripartite document that Craig, Stanley Baldwin and Cosgrave would sign on

3 December. The Free State and Northern Ireland were established and the Irish Question seemed finally if unsatisfactorily answered.

The legacy of the Civil War was a chasm in the political and sociological life of the new states; in the south it served as a dire litmus test for all in public life, whether national or local. The first decade of the Free State's existence was menaced by the existence of recently armed and undecommissioned bitter and disappointed men. De Valera's taming and politicising of a majority of these into his newly founded Fianna Fáil party was the greatest of his many services to his country. Cynics marvelled at how it managed to sidestep what a decade before had been the burning question of the oath of allegiance, and its leader proved that for twenty-six counties at least Collins' conviction that the Treaty terms gave the freedom to achieve freedom had been literally true. This was of small comfort to northern nationalists held in effective thraldom in a discriminatory and one-party state, but their fate had been partially waxed in 1916 by Lloyd George and finally sealed by the death of Michael Collins.

Were they needless deaths after all, those 927 fatalities? They were probably needless but were certainly inevitable given the quasi-religious nature of the struggle and the remarkable personalities of the participants. There is no given reason why the birth pangs of a new state should have been so exquisite or the delivery so bloody. Residual taunters can point to sixteen executions by the British after 1916 and twenty-four during the Anglo-Irish War and compare them with the seventy-seven killed by 'fellow Irishmen'. This kind of insensate rhetoric and the exaltation with which the 'armed struggle' fires its participants is with us still. History *does* teach and those who will not learn its lessons are often forced to endure it again.

CHRONOLOGY OF THE CIVIL WAR

1921

9 July: Truce brings to an end hostilities in Anglo-Irish War – comes into effect on 11 July

14–21 July: Lloyd George and de Valera hold exploratory meetings in London

6 December: 'Plenipotentiary' delegation led by Griffith and Collins signs Treaty

14 December: Dáil Éireann meets in UCD to debate the terms of the Treaty

15 December: De Valera's Document No. 2 offered to Dáil

19 December: Griffith introduces motion to accept Treaty terms; de Valera withdraws Document No. 2

1922

7 January: Dáil approves Griffith's motion (64–57)

9 January: De Valera resigns presidency

11 January: De Valera defeated in re-election for presidency (60–58) and Griffith elected; de Valera and supporters walk out

1 February: Pro-Treaty forces occupy Beggars Bush barracks

11 March: Anti-Treatyites cede control of Limerick to pro-Treaty troops

26 March: Banned Army Convention held in Mansion House

13 April: Anti-Treatyites occupy Four Courts, Kilmainham and buildings on the east side of O'Connell Street

20 May: Election pact announced by Collins and de Valera

14 June: Collins withdraws from pact under British pressure

16 June: General election, with greatly increased support for the Treaty

22 June: Shooting of Sir Henry Wilson in London

26 June: Kidnapping of General J. J. O'Connell, assistant chief of staff of pro-Treaty forces

28 June: Bombardment of Four Courts, marking the formal star: of the Civil War

5 July: Anti-Treatyite forces are defeated in O'Connell Street

12 August: Death of Arthur Griffith; William Cosgrave replaces him as head of the Provisional Government

22 August: Death of Michael Collins in an ambush in County Cork

10 October: Army Council proclamation indicating Special Emergency Powers granted by the Dáil

22 October: Irish hierarchy issues solemn pastoral letter against the anti-Treatyites

17 November: First government executions under Special Powers (by 2 May 1923 seventy-seven republicans were executed)

24 November: Erskine Childers shot by firing-squad while awaiting decision on appeal

30 November: Liam Lynch issues order that any TDs who voted for Special Powers measure are to be shot on sight

6 December: Irish Free State (Saorstát Éireann) comes into existence with Tim Healy as governor-general

7 December: Seán Hales, TD, shot dead by anti-Treatyite gunmen

8 December: Rory O'Connor, Liam Mellows and two other republican prisoners shot in Mountjoy in reprisal

1923

8 January: Eight Free State soldiers executed for 'treachery'

29 January: Liam Deasy signs document of 'unconditional surrender'

1 February: Army Council takes even more draconian powers,

extending the death penalty to the possession of subversive papers

7 March: Eight republican prisoners blown up by landmine at Ballyseedy Cross, County Kerry

24 March: At secret meeting in County Waterford de Valera's peace proposals defeated by six votes to five, largely at the instigation of Liam Lynch; four republican prisoners executed at Drumboe, near Stranorlar, County Donegal

10 April: Liam Lynch mortally wounded in Knockmealdown mountains

30 April: Frank Aiken, new chief of staff, declares a unilateral ceasefire

24 May: Aiken orders anti-Treatyites in the field to dump arms; de Valera issues his 'Legion of the Rearguard' proclamation

1924

July: Most anti-Treatyite internees, including de Valera, freed

8 November: General amnesty

1925

7 October : Sir James Craig repudiates in advance boundary commission's findings

3 December: Craig, Baldwin and Cosgrave sign the tripartite agreement that determines the border between Northern Ireland and the Free State

BIOGRAPHICAL INDEX

Frank Aiken (1898–1983) was born in Camlough, County Armagh, and became commandant of a division of the IRA in Ulster in 1921. He opposed the Treaty but tried to prevent the outbreak of war. His division engaged in sporadic activity in the mountains near Dundalk and when he became chief of staff of the anti-Treaty forces on the death of Liam Lynch in April 1923 he used his authority to call off hostilities and issued the order 'to dump arms' on 24 May. He became minister of defence in de Valera's first government and held office in each Fianna Fáil administration until 1969. He retired in 1973, having won great respect for Ireland at the United Nations.

Thomas Ashe (1885–1917) was born in Lispole, County Kerry and trained as a teacher, becoming the principal of Lusk NS in north County Dublin. He was active in the Gaelic League and was County Meath commander of the Volunteers. He featured in its greatest military success at the ambush of an RIC detachment at Ashbourne on the Friday of Easter Week. He was sentenced to life imprisonment but released in 1917. Rearrested, he organised a hunger-strike in Mountjoy for political status for Sinn Féin prisoners and died of pneumonia brought on by force-feeding.

Herbert Henry Asquith (1852–1928) was Liberal prime minister (1908–14) and led the war coalition until he was superseded by Lloyd George in 1916. The Rising found him at his weakest politically and he allowed Maxwell too much power in its aftermath.

Stanley Baldwin (1867–1947) was born in Bewdley, Worcestershire, and educated at Harrow and Trinity College, Cambridge. A steel millionaire, he succeeded Bonar Law as Conservative leader in 1923 and alternated with Ramsay Mac-

Donald as premier until his resignation in 1937, when he was made Earl Baldwin of Bewdley. He was unfairly blamed for Britain's state of military unreadiness in the face of the Nazi threat but was praised for his handling of the crisis over Edward VIII's abdication. He supported James Craig in the question of the Boundary Commission's findings in 1925 and was one of the signatories of the agreement which determined the border between Northern Ireland and the Free State.

Kevin Barry (1902–20) was born in Dublin and joined the Irish Volunteers in 1917 while still at Belvedere. On 20 September 1920, while a medical student at UCD, he took part in an ambush in which an even younger soldier was killed. Found hiding under a cart in possession of a revolver, Barry was sentenced to be hanged. His execution, on I November, prompted widespread criticism.

Tom Barry (1897–1980) was born in Rosscarbery, County Cork, the son of a policeman who had bought a pub on his retirement. He joined the army in 1915 and served at Ypres and later in Mesopotamia. Two years after the war he enrolled in a business college in Cork but was approached by Volunteers as a man of known military experience. Soon he had trained his own highly disciplined West Cork flying column – a concept in guerrilla warfare he largely developed himself. In November 1920 he led the Kilmichael ambush, in which the Auxiliaries suffered their most serious defeat, and on March 1921 at Crossbarry successfully engaged a superior force from the Essex regiment. He took the anti-Treaty side in the Civil War and continued as a member of the IRA until 1938, when he resigned because he disagreed with the organisation's bombing campaign in Britain. He subsequently published *Guerrilla Days in Ireland* (1949), an inevitably partisan account of his activities as a flying-column leader.

Robert Barton (1881–1975), a cousin of Erskine Childers, was born in County Wicklow and educated at Rugby and Oxford. He resigned from the British army in 1916 and joined the IRA. minister for agriculture in the first Dáil, he worked out the terms of the truce which ended the War of Independence in 1921. He was one of the signatories of the Treaty, recommending it as 'the lesser of two outrages', but remained a supporter of de Valera. He was chairman of the Agricultural Credit Corporation (1934–54) and later of Bord na Móna.

Piaras Beaslaí (1881–1965) was born in Liverpool and moved to Dublin in 1904. He was active in the Gaelic League and did much to politicise it. He commanded the forces in the North King Street area during the Rising and was editor of *An tÓglach* and IRA director of publicity from February 1921. He supported the treaty and served as commandant general in the Free State army. Resigning in 1924, he became a writer and Gaelic scholar, and Michael Collins' first biographer.

Augustine Birrell (1850–1933) was born near Liverpool. He was chief secretary for Ireland (1907–16) and was tireless in his efforts to keep the spirit of the Home Rule bill alive. He resigned after the Rising and saw all his sound advice wantonly ignored.

Harry Boland (1887–1922) was born in Dublin and became secretary of Sinn Féin in 1917. He was one of Collins' closest friends, was active in the IRB and served as a TD in the first Dáil. He took the anti-Treaty side during the Civil War and was shot while being arrested at Skerries on 31 July 1922.

Dan Breen (1894–1969) was a farmer's son, born in Soloheadbeg, County Tipperary, the scene of the attack on a party of RIC men – in which he and Seán Treacy were involved – on 21 January 1919 that is taken as being the first action in the War of Independence. They were also active in Dublin, making an attempt on the life of the lord lieutenant, among other things. He continued guerrilla activity in Tipperary during the Civil War until he was captured on 17 April 1923. He was the first opponent of the Treaty to sit in the Dáil, taking his seat in January 1927. He served as Fianna Fáil TD for Tipperary South from 1932 to 1965. His autobiography, *My Fight for Irish Freedom* (1924), contains a rather subjective account of his guerrilla years.

Ned Broy (1887–1972) was born in County Kildare and worked as a sergeant-clerk in the DMP from 1911. He became one of Collins' most successful agents in the Castle, supplying him with early information about police intentions. He was arrested in February 1921 and jailed for six months. After the Treaty, he was made an adjutant in the air force and promoted to colonel. He succeeded Eoin O'Duffy as commissioner of the gardaí and formed an armed group of police to aid the confiscation of cattle from farmers who refused to pay rates; this group became known as 'Broy's Harriers'. He was always interested in athletics and became president of the Irish Olympic Council in 1935.

Cathal Brugha (1874–1922) was born Charles Burgess in Dublin. He joined the Gaelic League in 1899 and the Volunteers in 1913. He was second in command to Eamonn Ceannt in the South Dublin Union in Easter week and was so badly wounded on the Thursday that he was permanently crippled. He was a strong opponent of the Treaty and was shot in Talbot Street in the second week of the Civil War.

Roger Casement (1864–1916) was born in Dublin of County Antrim parents and educated at Ballymena Academy. He joined the British consular service in 1892 and was knighted for his reports on human rights violations in the Congo and the Amazon basin. He joined the Gaelic League in 1904 and the Volunteers in 1913. Arrested off the County Kerry coast at Easter 1916 on his return from Germany, he was hanged in Pentonville on 3 August 1916, having been received into the Catholic church.

Eamonn Ceannt (1881–1916) was born Edmund Kent in Glenamaddy, County Galway. He commanded the South Dublin Union, a post that was fiercely attacked but did not fall. He was bitterly disappointed by Pearse's surrender. He was shot by firing squad on 8 May 1916.

Erskine Childers (1870–1922) was born in London but was reared in Wicklow. He was educated at Haileybury and Cambridge and saw service in the Boer War. An expert mariner (his novel *The Riddle of the Sands*, postulating a German invasion of Britain, was a bestseller in 1903 and has never been out of print since), he brought a shipment of arms for the Irish Volunteers into Howth in July 1914. He served in the royal navy air service during the Great War and suc-

ceeded Desmond Fitzgerald as director of publicity for the
Volunteers during the War of Independence, editing the
highly propagandist and extremely successful *Irish Bulletin*.
Though a member of the Treaty delegation, he rejected the
Treaty's terms and was executed by firing squad by government forces on 24 November 1922 for being in possession of
a revolver, a gift from his friend Michael Collins.

Sir Winston Churchill OM (1874–1965) was the eldest son
of Lord Randolph Churchill and born in Blenheim Palace,
the home of his grander relation, the Duke of Marlborough.
While minister of war and air in Lloyd George's coalition
(1918– 21), he advocated the criminalisation of IRA activities, refusing to regard them as a legitimate army at war, but
he was an active member of the Treaty negotiations and
strongly supported the Free State. After many years as a
political maverick he became prime minister on the fall of
Neville Chamberlain and was one of the significant leaders in
the Second World War. He refused all royal honours except
the exclusive Order of Merit until his late acceptance of a
knighthood. He won the Nobel Prize for Literature in 1953.

Kathleen Clarke (1879–1972) was born Daly in Limerick, where
she married Tom Clarke on his release from prison in 1898.
She became formal head of the IRB when the leaders were
executed and initiated an Irish Volunteers Dependants Fund
within a few days of the executions. She helped to organise
Cumann na mBan in 1921, opposed the Treaty and was
Dublin's first woman Lord Mayor (in 1939).

Thomas James Clarke (1857–1916) was born in the Isle of
Wight of Irish parents and brought up in South Africa and
Dungannon. He went to America in 1871 and joined Clan
na Gael, returning to England on a dynamiting mission in
1883. He was arrested and sentenced to life imprisonment, of
which he served fifteen years under severe conditions. He was
released in 1898 but unable to find work, returned to the US.
His return to Dublin in 1907 was with the deliberate intention of reviving the IRB. A signatory of the Proclamation,
he served in the GPO during Easter Week and was executed
with Pearse and MacDonagh on 3 May 1916.

Con Colbert (1893–1916) was a member of Na Fianna and later joined the IRB and the Irish Volunteers. In the Easter Rising he commanded the post in Watkin's Brewery in Ardee Street. He was executed in Kilmainham on 8 May 1916.

Michael Collins (1890–1922) was born in Clonakilty, County Cork, and served as a clerk in the British civil service in London. He joined the IRB in 1915 and was one of the survivors of Easter Week. By the time he was released from Frongoch in December 1916 he was already an important leader in the movement and he played an important part its reorganisation. During the War of Independence he was a brilliant if ruthless head of military intelligence. He was a reluctant member of the Treaty delegation but regarded the terms as the best that were possible in the circumstances. Though he had little experience of actual guerrilla fighting, he was the obvious choice for commander in chief of the Free State forces during the Civil War. He was killed in an ambush in Béal na mBláth, not far from his birthplace, on 22 August 1922.

James Connolly (1868–1916) was born in Edinburgh of Irish parents. Having been a socialist labour organiser in Ireland and the US, he returned to Ireland in 1910 and was the worker's leader while Larkin was imprisoned during the 1913 lock-out. He formed the Citizen Army, convinced that Ireland was ripe for an armed socialist revolt. He was persuaded to join with the IRB and as the leader with some experience was made military commander during the Rising. His execution on 12 May 1916 marked the end of the judicial killings.

Sir Alfred Cope (1880–1954), known popularly as 'Andy', was a career politician and served as assistant under-secretary to Sir Hamar Greenwood during the War of Independence. He was one of the most active and successful parties in bringing about the Truce that finished the war and he assisted General Macready in supervising the withdrawal of British troops. He was knighted in 1922.

William Cosgrave (1880–1965) was born in Dublin and was active as a Sinn Féin councillor. He was adjutant to Eamonn

Ceannt in the South Dublin Union in Easter Week but a death sentence against him was commuted and he was released under the general amnesty. He replaced Arthur Griffith as chairman of the Provisional Government in August 1922 and had the responsibility of carrying on the Civil War, which he did with great distress and an equally stern sense of duty. His was the sure if conservative hand that shaped and stabilised the new Free State; during his years of office he had to face continuing republican activity, a mutiny in the army and the loss of his brilliant and enigmatic minister for justice, Kevin O'Higgins. He was one of the founders of Fine Gael (1933) and its leader from 1935 until his retirement in 1944.

James Craig (1871–1940) was born in Belfast and educated in Edinburgh. He was Edward Carson's lieutenant during the anti-Home Rule agitation in 1913 and leader of the Ulster unionists at the founding of the Northern Ireland state in 1921, becoming its first prime minister. He made sure of local and provincial unionist political domination by the abolition of proportional representation in 1929 and effectively neutered the boundary commission by threats, non-cooperation and the fact that he was confident of support from Stanley Baldwin, the British prime minister. Though instinctively less sectarian that some of his cabinet colleagues, he made no effort to curb their anti-Catholic legislation. Knighted in 1918, he was created Viscount Craigavon in 1927.

Frank Percy Crozier (1879–1937) was a dashing career soldier of Ulster extraction who fought in both the Boer War and the Great War, training the UVF in the interval. He rose to the rank of brigadier and was active in both the Lithuanian and Polish armies against the Bolsheviks. He assumed command of the Auxiliary cadets but resigned in February 1921 when his attempts to discipline the force were frustrated by General Tudor. He wrote a number of books of memoirs, including *Ireland for Ever* (1932), which was remarkably pro-nationalist.

Edward Daly (1891–1916) was born in Limerick into a noted Republican family. His sister Kathleen married Tom Clarke. He joined the Volunteers in 1914 and commanded the Four

Courts garrison during Easter Week. He was executed in Kilmainham on 4 May 1916.

Éamon de Valera (1882–1975) was born in New York but was brought up in County Limerick from the age of two. He became a lecturer in mathematics and joined the Gaelic League in 1908 and the Volunteers in 1914. Commander at Boland's Mills during Easter Week, he was the only 1916 leader to survive a sentence of execution, largely due to the efforts of John Redmond and John Dillon. He was president of the first Dáil Éireann and the first leader to meet Lloyd George after the truce which ended the Anglo-Irish War in 1921. He refused to lead the Treaty delegation and rejected the terms agreed by Collins and Griffith. Largely inactive during the Civil War, he signed the order of cessation of hostilities in 1923. His greatest postwar achievement was the politicisation of the republican movement by the founding of the Fianna Fáil party, which he led as Taoiseach in four governments. He also served two terms as president (1959–73).

Liam Deasy (1898–1974) was born near Bandon, County Cork, and was adjutant of the West Cork brigade of the IRA during the Anglo-Irish War. He rejected the Treaty and though he fought in the Civil War was greatly distressed by its effects. He believed that the surrender of the Four Courts should have meant the end rather than the beginning of hostilities. He was captured by government forces in January 1923 and, convinced that the time had come to end the fighting, signed a document worded for him by his captors that he was in favour of unconditional surrender. After the war he took no further part in public life but served throughout the Emergency in the Irish army. He published an account of the brigade's activities, *Towards Ireland Free,* and a book on the Civil War, *Brother against Brother.*

John Devoy (1842–1928) was born in Kill, County Kildare, and served in both the French Foreign Legion and the British army, where he became a Fenian spy. He helped in the rescue of the Fenian 'chief' James Stephens from Richmond Jail in 1865 and, given fifteen years imprisonment for organising 'cells', was amnestied having served five years on condition of his living outside the United Kingdom. He led Clan na Gael and supported all anti-British movements thereafter, including the Land War and the Rising. He died penniless in Atlantic City.

John Dillon (1851–1927) was an often violent supporter of Parnell but led the anti-Parnellites after the split. In the aftermath of the Rising he was active in pleading for an end to the arrests and executions.

Éamonn Duggan (1874–1936) was born in County Meath and qualified as a solicitor in 1914. He was arrested after the Easter Rising and became director of IRA intelligence. He was elected to the first Dáil in 1918; he was imprisoned in 1920 but was subsequently released, to take part in the Mansion House talks that led to the Truce. He was one of the signatories of the Treaty and held several posts in Cosgrave's government, retiring in 1933 to become a senator.

Madeleine ffrench-Mullen (1880–1944) was a member of Inghinidhe na hÉireann and children's editor of its newspaper *Bean na hÉireann* (1908–11). A member of the Citizen Army she was in charge of the medical post in the College of Surgeons, and in 1919 helped found St Ultan's Infant Hospital with her friend Kathleen Lynn.

John Denton French, First Earl of Ypres (1852–1925) was born in Kent into a family with property in County Roscommon. He joined the royal navy when he was fourteen but later transferred to the army. After a successful career as a cavalry officer in the Sudan and during the Boer War, he became chief inspector of the garda síochána in 1911. Forced to resign because of his support for the anti-Home Rule officers in the Curragh, he was recalled to lead the British Expeditionary Force in 1914, when the Great War began. General Douglas Haig replaced him because of his lack of diplomatic skills and his inability to liaise with the French army. He was made lord lieutenant of Ireland in 1918, resigning in 1921 with a gratuity of £50,000 after a period of office in which he demonstrated his lack of understanding of the Irish situation. During this period many attempts were made on his life, the most dangerous one involving the Squad, with Dan Breen and Seán Treacy, on 19 December 1919.

Frank Gallagher (1893–1962) was born in Cork and was deputy to Erskine Childers on the staff of the Volunteer propaganda news-sheet the *Irish Bulletin*, which presented the activities of the IRA in the best possible light and was extremely influential in winning international support for the Irish cause. He was the first editor of the *Irish Press* (1931–95) and later worked for Radio Éireann and the National Library.

David Lloyd George (1863–1945) was born in Manchester but was brought up in Criccieth in Gwynedd. He had a brilliant career as a Liberal reformer, associated with old-age pensions, National Insurance and the taming of the House of Lords. He was minister of munitions, secretary for war and, having ousted Asquith, prime minister from 1916, proving a highly efficient war leader. Usually in sympathy with the Ulster unionists, he decided on exclusion on their terms as early as 1916, and his dealings with the nationalist Irish were vitiated by the instinctive and deep suspicion of one Celtic race for another. Slow to give the War of Independence the political attention it deserved, he tried an ineffectual mixture of conciliation and coercion until forced to seek an end to the struggle through the truce. It was his threat of 'war within three days' that persuaded Griffith and Collins to accept the Treaty terms. The 'Irish Question' helped force his resignation as prime minister in 1922.

Sir Hamar Greenwood (1870–1948) was born in Canada and came to live in England in 1895. He was called to the bar in 1906 and was elected as a Liberal MP in the same year. He took silk in 1910 and served in France in the Great War (1914–16). He was appointed chief secretary to Ireland on 12 April 1920 and, though it caused him some private embarrassment, he publicly defended the excesses of the Tans and Auxiliaries. He took little part in the pre-truce talks, though he was present during the Treaty negotiations. Made a baronet in 1915, he followed Churchill to join the Conservative Party and became a viscount in 1937.

Arthur Griffith (1871–1922) was born in Dublin and became a journalist, a member of the Gaelic League and the IRB.

With Bulmer Hobson, he founded Sinn Féin, which advocated Irish self-sufficiency and passive resistance as the best means of ending British Rule. He opposed the Home Rule bill of 1914 and was arrested after the Easter Rising, although he had not been a participant in it. Released at the general amnesty, he was re-arrested at the time of the 'German Plot' in 1918. He was elected MP for East Cavan while still in prison and was acting president of the Dáil while de Valera was in America (1919–20). He was arrested in November 1920 but was released shortly before the truce in July 1921. He led the Treaty delegation in December of that year and was its first signatory. Elected president of the Dáil when de Valera resigned, he died of a cerebral haemorrhage on 12 August 1922, worn out by the strain of.the negotiations and the Civil War which greeted the rejection of the Treaty terms.

Seán Heuston (1891–1916) joined the Volunteers in 1913 and led a contingent of Na Fianna to bring arms from the *Asgard* safely to Dublin. He was in command of the Mendicity Institute but had to surrender on the Wednesday of Easter Week. He was executed in Kilmainham on 8 May 1916.

Bulmer Hobson (1883–1969) with Denis McCullough founded the Dungannon clubs which helped to resuscitate the IRB. He was also a member of the GAA, the Gaelic League, Griffith's Sinn Féin and founder of the Ulster Literary Theatre. He disapproved of the planned Rising and was kept in detention until the fighting had begun.

Thomas Kent (c. 1867–1916) was a Volunteer who awaited the countermanding of MacNeill's orders in his home in Cork. On 2 May 1916 his house was surrounded by the RIC attempting to arrest him; he and his brothers resisted, holding out for three hours, during which a head constable and one of the Kent brothers were shot. He was executed in Cork seven days later.

Andrew Bonar Law (1858–1923) was born in Canada but worked as an iron merchant in Glasgow, serving as a Unionist MP from 1910. He replaced Arthur Balfour as unionist leader in the House of Commons. He actively supported Ulster's resistance to Home Rule and left Lloyd George with little room to manoeuvre during the Treaty negotiations. He replaced him as prime minister (1922–3).

Seán Lemass (1899–1971) was born in Ballybrack, County Dublin, and as a fifteen-year-old fought in the GPO in 1916. He opposed the Treaty and was active in the Wicklow Mountains after the surrender of the Four Courts. Interned in 1923, he decided that the republican ideal must be attained by political means rather than by force of arms. He was one of the architects of the Fianna Fáil party and was foremost in developing Ireland's potential as a modern European nation. He served as taoiseach from 1959–66 and in 1965 made the significant offer of friendship to Terence O'Neill, then Stormont prime minister.

Brig. General William Henry Muir Lowe (1861–c. 1940) was the commander of British forces in Dublin during Easter Week, until Maxwell became military governor on the Friday. He received Pearse's surrender and was mentioned in dispatches, being promoted to the honorary rank of major general.

Liam Lynch (1893–1923) was born in County Limerick and worked in a hardware business until 1919, when he organised the Cork Volunteers. He then became an able brigade commander during the Anglo-Irish War. He opposed the Treaty and was anxious to avoid a conflict but after the beginning of the Civil War became the most implacable of commanders. He led the southern division of the anti-Treatyites and hoped to hold a 'Munster Republic' against the Free State forces. He was mortally wounded in the Knockmealdown mountains in County Waterford on 10 April 1923.

Kathleen Florence Lynn (1874–1955) was a suffragist and feminist. She joined the Citizen Army and became its chief medical officer, negotiating the surrender of City Hall. She became an executive member of Sinn Féin in 1918 and opposed the Treaty.

John MacBride (1865–1916) joined the IRB and worked with Michael Cusack in the formation of the GAA. He served as a major with the Boers in the Boer War. He was not a member of the Volunteers but the offer of his services was gladly accepted by MacDonagh, who made him second in command at Jacob's. He was shot by firing squad in Kilmainham on 5 May 1916.

Tomás MacCurtain (1884–1920) was born in County Cork and was a member (and teacher) in the Gaelic League and, with Terence MacSwiney, organised the Cork Volunteers in preparation for the Easter Rising. After his release from internment, he was active in the movement, becoming the first Sinn Féin lord mayor of Cork. He was assassinated by a gang of masked raiders – almost certainly Black and Tans. The coroner's verdict blamed, among others, Lloyd George and DI Swanzy for his death.

Seán MacDermott (1884–1916) while working as a barmen in Belfast met Bulmer Hobson, under whose influence he joined the IRB and in 1907 became a full-time organiser for Sinn Féin. He was probably the best organiser and had the most determined mind of all the leaders, devising with Plunkett a forged document that suggested that the authorities were about to proscribe the Volunteers. He fought in the GPO and on 12 May 1916 was the penultimate insurgent to be executed.

Thomas MacDonagh (1878–1916) joined the Gaelic League in 1901 and helped Pearse to establish St Enda's in 1908. He was a founder member of the Irish Volunteers in 1913 and its director of training. He joined the IRB on cooption to the military council and commanded the garrison at Jacob's factory in Bishop Street. He was executed on 3 May 1916, along with Pearse and Clarke.

Seán MacEntee (1889–1984) as commander of the County Louth division was held responsible for the deaths of two prisoners. He was condemned to death but the sentence was commuted to life imprisonment. Released in 1917, he fought in the Anglo-Irish war and opposed the Treaty. A founder member of Fianna Fáil, he held many cabinet posts, his last as minister for health (1957–65).

Seán MacEoin (1894–1973), known as the 'Blacksmith of Ballinalee' (in County Longford), led a flying column there during the Anglo-Irish War. He supported the Treaty and became chief of staff of the Free State army. He resigned in

1929 to become a TD and served as Fine Gael minister in both the inter-party governments. He stood unsuccessfully for the presidency in 1945 and 1959.

Sir Cecil Francis Neville Macready (1862–1945) was born in Aberdeen, the son of the great Shakespearean actor William Macready (1793–1873), himself of Irish extraction, who sired him at age sixty-four. He joined the Gordon Highlanders and was GOC Belfast before becoming adjutant to Lord French in the British Expeditionary Force. Promoted to brigadier rank in 1918, he served as commissioner of the Metropolitan Police (1918–20) before being persuaded to accept the post of general officer commanding in Ireland by his old commander, Lord French. Though disclaiming any trace of Irishness, his code of military conduct made him publicly decry the behaviour of the Black and Tans and the Auxies. He was active in seeking the basis for a truce, was present at discussions with de Valera, Griffith and Jan Christian Smuts in July 1921 and worked out the terms of the Truce with Robert Barton and Eamonn Duggan. He oversaw the withdrawal of British forces in January 1922 and retired from the army in 1923.

Terence MacSwiney (1879–1920) was born in Cork and, with Tomás Mac Curtain organised the Volunteers in anticipation of the Easter Rising. He succeeded MacCurtain as lord mayor of Cork after the latter's death in March 1920. Arrested under the Defence of the Realm Act on 19 August 1920, he went on hunger strike in Brixton. He died on 24 October after seventy-four days on hunger strike, during which all appeals for his release had gone unheeded, but the publicity surrounding his protracted death was very damaging to Britain's reputation in Europe, Australia and America. His funeral in London had a guard of honour of Volunteers in prohibited uniform and the streets were filled with mourners, not all of them Irish exiles.

Denis McCullough (1883–1968) was a close associate of Bulmer Hobson in the founding of the Dungannon Clubs and the Ulster Literary Theatre, and became president of the IRB. He helped to organise the Volunteers in Ulster and was arrested in 1916 and interned at Frongoch.

Eoin MacNeill (1867–1945) was professor of early Irish history in UCD (1908–45) and was a leading force in the founding of the Irish Volunteers. He was opposed to the Rising as planned and tried with some success to prevent the Volunteers form mobilising. Later he supported the Treaty, becoming minister of education in the first Free State Dáil.

Michael Mallin (1880–1916) was born in Dublin. He was in command in St Stephen's Green but soon realised that an occupied Shelbourne Hotel would dominate the fire and the company retired to the College of Surgeons. He was shot in Kilmainham on 8 May 1916.

Constance Markievicz (1868–1927) was born Gore-Booth in London and brought up at Lissadell, County Sligo, where her Protestant ascendancy family had extensive estates. She joined the Citizen Army and was second in command to Mallin in the St Stephen's Green sector. She was condemned to death but on the sentence's commutation to penal servitude for life was kept in Aylesbury prison in Buckinghamshire until the amnesty in 1917. In the 1918 general election she was elected for St Patrick's division, Dublin – the first woman MP – but did not take her seat. She opposed the Treaty and toured America to enlist support for the republican cause. She died shortly after election to the Dáil as a Fianna Fáil TD.

General Sir John Maxwell (1859–1929) became commander in chief, Ireland, superseding Lowe on 28 April 1916. He insisted upon a complete and urgent defeat for the Volunteers. Instigating martial law, he was the only authority in Ireland for the next critical month and the policy of paced executions and massive arrests was his. When the British government realised the effects of his policies they did what they could to mitigate them.

Liam Mellows (1892–1922) was born in Manchester but reared in County Wexford. He was a member of Fianna Éireann (the youth organisation of the Volunteers), was strongly influenced by the views of James Connolly (1868–1916) and fought in minor actions in Galway during Easter Week. He escaped to America, where he worked with John Devoy on the

Gaelic American and organised de Valera's eighteen-month fund-raising tour of America (1919–20). IRA director of purchases, he considered the Treaty a betrayal of the republic and wished to establish a revolutionary counter to the Provisional Government. He was part of the Four Courts garrison and, like his comrade Rory O'Connor, was executed in Mountjoy on 8 December 1922, the day after the assassination of Seán Hales, TD, a member of the government, as a deterrent against further killings of public representatives.

Helena Molony (1884–1967) was born in Dublin and joined Inghinidhe na hÉireann in 1903, becoming editor of its newspaper *Bean na hÉireann* in 1908. She was given the task by Connolly in 1915 of organising the Irish Women Workers Union (IWWU) and was with the City Hall command during Easter Week. She was released in December 1916, continued her trade-union work and was president of ICTU (1922–3).

Richard Mulcahy (1886–1971) was born in Waterford and worked as a post-office clerk. He was involved in the ambush at Ashbourne during Easter Week and after the general amnesty became a senior figure in the IRA. He supported the Treaty and as commander in chief after Collins' death was vigorous in his activity against the anti-Treatyites. He was one of the founders of the Fine Gael party in 1933 and, precluded because of his Civil War reputation from the post of taoiseach in the coalition governments of the 1940s and 1950s, served as minister of education under John A. Costello.

Rory O'Connor (1883–1922) was born in Dublin and worked as a railway engineer in Canada. Interned after the Easter Rising, he was director of engineering during the Anglo-Irish War and became a leader of the anti-Treatyites, the members of the IRA who were determined to fight against the agreement. He set up the republican garrison in the Four Courts in April 1922 and was arrested at its surrender in June. He was executed on 8 December in Mountjoy with three other republicans – Liam Mellows, Richard Barrett and Joseph McKelvey – as a reprisal for the killing, the previous day, of

Seán Hales, TD, a member of the Provisional Government, and as a deterrent against similar assassinations of public representatives.

Jeremiah O'Donovan Rossa (1831–1915) was born in Ross-carbery, County Cork, the 'Rossa' being added to his name for effect. He was one of the early Fenian organisers, founding the Phoenix Society of Skibbereen in 1858. He had the usual Fenian career of nationalist activity, 'seditious' journalism, appalling treatment in British prisons and political exile. Because of his abrasive personality and alcoholism he was often at odds with the other members of Clan na Gael. At his funeral in Glasnevin, Pearse claimed him as a symbol of IRB continuity.

Eoin O'Duffy (1892–1944) was born near Castleblayney, County Monaghan, and trained as an engineer. He fought in the Anglo-Irish War, becoming chief of staff of the IRA in succession to Richard Mulcahy. He supported the Treaty and became commissioner of the garda síochána. He was dismissed from the post in 1933 when de Valera became taoiseach and in July that year formed the Army Comrades' Association. The name of the group was changed to the National Guard and it was intended as a protective force for the Fine Gael party against the attacks of Fianna Fáil supporters. With their fascist trappings and distinctive uniforms, the members became known as the 'Blueshirts'. William Cosgrave disapproved of the National Guard's undemocratic aura and the movement gradually disintegrated. In 1936 O'Duffy organised an Irish Brigade to fight for Franco in the Spanish Civil War, in spite of Ireland's official policy of non-interference. When he died on 30 November 1944 he was given a state funeral.

Michael O'Hanrahan (1877–1916) was born in New Ross, County Wexford. He joined the Volunteers in 1913 and was with MacDonagh in Jacob's factory during the Rising. He was executed on 4 May 1916.

Kevin O'Higgins (1892–1927) was born in Stradbally, Queen's County [Laois], and educated at Clongowes, Maynooth and UCD. He joined Sinn Féin and was imprisoned for making an anti-conscription speech in 1918. He was a strong Treatyite and the architect of the garda síochána, the acceptable civilian police force, and he took vigorous measures to restore law and order to a war-torn country. He drew up the list of special powers arrogated by the army in October 1922 and was one of the signatories of the order to execute Rory O'Connor (who had been his best man), Liam Mellows and two others in exemplary reprisal for the shooting of Seán Hales, TD. This was the probable cause of the shooting of his father in February 1923 and of his own killing by republicans in July 1927.

Ernie O'Malley (1898–1957) was born in Castlebar and was a medical student in UCD when he fought in Easter Week. He was active during the Anglo-Irish War and, opposing the Treaty, was appointed a member of the IRA Army Council in October 1922. He was badly wounded and captured by government forces in November 1922; having recovered from his wounds he went on a hunger strike which lasted for forty-one days in Mountjoy. His death sentence was commuted when the surgeons said he would never walk again. He was elected abstentionist TD for North Dublin in 1923 and released in July 1924. Having recovered the use of his limbs he travelled widely and was one of the chief fund-raisers for the *Irish Press*. His accounts of his experiences in the Anglo-Irish War – *On Another Man's Wound* (1936) – and the Civil War – *The Singing Flame* (1978) – are regarded as the finest literary record of the events of the two conflicts.

The O'Rahilly (1875–1916) was born Michael Joseph Rahilly in Ballylongford, County Kerry. He was a member of Sinn Féin and joined the Volunteers in 1913, becoming its director of arms. He helped MacNeill call off the Rising but went to Dublin himself. He was killed during the retreat from the GPO to Moore Street on the Friday of Easter Week.

Patrick Henry Pearse (1879–1916) joined the Gaelic League in 1895 and incorporated many of its ideals and techniques in his school, St Enda's, begun in 1908. He had been editor of *An Claidheamh Soluis* (1903–9) and had already begun in his writings to talk of a cleansing blood sacrifice which would restore the quick heart of Irish nationalism. He was commander in chief of the forces in the Rising, president of the provisional government, part-author with Connolly and MacDonagh (and one of the signatories) of the Proclamation which he read to a largely uninterested Dublin audience on Easter Monday and the person who agreed to unconditional surrender on Saturday 29 April 1916. He was the first to be executed four days later.

William Pearse (1881–1916) was born in Dublin, the brother of Patrick whom he greatly admired. He was a fine sculptor and art master at St Enda's. He was a captain in the GPO but in no way involved in the planning of the Rising. His execution on 4 May 1916 was unquestionably due to the notoriety of his brother.

Joseph Mary Plunkett (1887–1916) was born in Dublin. He joined the Volunteers and was one of the first to be a member of the military council. He tried to assist Casement in Germany in a quest for arms in 1915 but concealed the fact that Casement had strongly advised against a rising. He was in the GPO during Easter Week and executed on 4 May after a prison marriage to the artist Grace Gifford.

John Redmond (1856–1918) was born in County Wexford. He became chairman of the Nationalist party in 1900, having healed the rift caused by the fall of Parnell. Holding the balance in the Commons in 1910, he was able to get Asquith to introduce a Home Rule bill. He encouraged recruitment in the British army and briefly supported Asquith's decision to make an example of the ringleaders of the Rising. His party was soundly defeated in the 1918 general election.

Francis Sheehy-Skeffington (1878–1916) was a well known supporter of such causes as women's suffrage, feminism and pacifism. He opposed the Rising and was arrested by Bowen-Colthurst and shot with Thomas Dickson and Patrick McIntyre in Portobello barracks on 26 April 1916.

Hanna Sheehy-Skeffington (1877–1946) was born Sheehy in Tipperary and educated at the Royal University. She married Francis Skeffington and joined with him in the campaign for women's suffrage. She was a messenger at the GPO in 1916 and refused £10,000 compensation for the murder of her husband. She later served as a judge in the Dáil courts.

Margaret Skinnider (c. 1893–1971) was born in Glasgow. She was one of Markievicz's battalion at St Stephen's Green and as a suffragist and feminist insisted in active participation in the fighting. A crack shot, she was a successful sniper until she was badly wounded and eventually arrested in St Vincent's Hospital.

Jan Christian Smuts (1870–1950) was born in Cape Colony and led the guerrilla forces in the Boer War (1899–1902). He was a key figure in the peace negotiations and in the setting up of the Union of South Africa in 1910. He served in the British war cabinets in both world wars but was unable to overcome the rise of Afrikaans nationalism. The defeat of his pro-Commonwealth United Party by the National Party in 1948 led, in 1967, to the setting up of the union as a republic outside the commonwealth. He was one of the prime movers in arranging the truce that ended the war in 1921 and is credited as the main architect of the speech of George V at the opening of the Northern Ireland parliament on 22 June 1921 that helped persuade the British to make every effort to secure a cessation.

Austin Stack (1879–1929) was born near Tralee, County Kerry, and was arrested for his involvement in the attempted landing of arms by Sir Roger Casement (1864–1916) at Banna Strand in April 1916. He was minister for home affairs in the first Dáil and a member of the Treaty delegation. He rejected the terms of the Treaty and was active in the Civil War until his capture in April 1923. During his imprisonment in Kilmainham he led a hunger strike for forty-one days, an ordeal from which his health never recovered.

Oscar Traynor (1886–1963) was born in Dublin and trained as a wood-carver and compositor. He took part in the 1916 Rising and was interned at Frongoch. Commander of the Dublin brigade of the IRA, he led the attack on the Customs House on 25 May 1921. He opposed the Treaty and continued to organise military activity in Wicklow after the battle for Dublin. He served in most Fianna Fáil governments until his resignation because of ill-health in 1961. A noted footballer, he played for Belfast Celtic when he was a young man and was president of the FAI from 1948 until his death.

Seán Treacy (1895–1920) was a leading Gaelic League organiser in South Tipperary and a member of the Irish Volunteers. With Dan Breen he led the Soloheadbeg ambush that began the War of Independence. He and Breen were involved in an attempt to assassinate the Viceroy, Lord French, in Dublin in December 1919. He was killed in a gun battle in Talbot Street, Dublin, on 14 October 1920.

Hugh H. Tudor (1871–1965) was born in Exeter and was wounded in action in both the Boer and the Great Wars. Appointed chief of the Irish police services in 1920, holding his military rank of major general, he oversaw the enlargement of the RIC with Black and Tans and Auxiliary cadets. He was constant in his defence of the new recruits but admitted that there was much drunkenness and indiscipline among them, blaming it on the conditions under which they had to operate. He initiated the use of the aeroplane as a counter-terrorist weapon and was subsequently air vice marshal and general officer commanding in Palestine, bringing with him many of his execrated personnel.

William Butler Yeats (1865–1939) was born in Dublin. He fell in love with Maud Gonne and through her was introduced to nationalism and IRB membership. He was deeply affected by the Rising, returning to it again and again in his poetry.

SELECT BIBLIOGRAPHY

Abbott, R. *Police Casualties in Ireland*. 1919–1922. Dublin & Cork, 2000.

Barry T. *Guerrilla Days in Ireland*. Cork, 1958.

Beckett, J. C. *The Making of Modern Ireland*. 1603–1923. London, 1966.

Breen, D. *My Fight for Irish Freedom*, Dublin, 1924 (revised 1964).

Brown, M. *The Politics of Irish Literature*. London, 1971.

Coffey, T. M. *Agony at Easter*. London, 1970.

Connolly, S (ed.). *The Oxford Companion to Irish History*. Oxford, 1998.

Coogan, T. P. *Michael Collins*. London, 1990.

Deasy, L. *Brother against Brother*. Cork, 1998.

—— *Towards Ireland Free*. Cork, 1973.

Department of External Affairs. *Cuimhneachán 1916–1966*. Dublin, 1966.

Doherty, G. and Keogh, D. (eds.) *Michael Collins and the Making of the Irish State*. Dublin, 1998.

Doherty, J. E. & Hickey, D. J. *A Chronology of Irish History since 1500*. Dublin, 1989.

Dwyer, T. Ryle. *De Valera: The Man and the Myths*. Dublin, 1991.

—— *Michael Collins: 'The Man Who Won the War'*. Cork, 1990.

Fanning, R. *Independent Ireland*. Dublin, 1983.

Foster, R. F. *Modern Ireland 1600–1972*. London, 1988.

—— (ed.) *The Oxford History of Ireland*. Oxford, 1989

Griffith, K. and O'Grady, T. (eds.) *Curious Journey*. Cork, 1998.

Hart, P. *The IRA and Its Enemies*. Oxford, 1998.

Kee, R. *The Green Flag*. London, 1970.

Kiberd, D. *Inventing Ireland*. London, 1995.

Lee, J. J. *Ireland 1912–1985*. Cambridge, 1989.

Lyons, F. S. L. *Ireland since the Famine*. London, 1971.

Mac Lochlainn, P. F. *Last Words*. Dublin, 1971.

Macardle, D. *The Irish Republic*. Dublin, 1937 (revised 1968).

McHugh, R. (ed.) *Dublin 1916*. London, 1966.

Neeson, E. *The Civil War 1922–23*. Dublin, 1989.

Neligan, D. *The Spy in the Castle*. London, 1968.

Ó Gadhra, N. *Civil War in Connacht 1922–1923*. Cork, 1999.

O'Malley, E. *On Another Man's Wound*. Dublin, 1936.

——— *The Singing Flame*. Dublin, 1978.

Ryan, D. *The Rising*. Dublin, 1949.

Welch, R. (ed.) *The Oxford Companion to Irish Literature*. Oxford, 1996.

INDEX

OTHER INTERESTING BOOKS

Tom Barry – IRA Freedom Fighter
Meda Ryan

This book chronicles the action-packed life of the Commander of the Third West Cork Flying Column and one of the great architects of modern guerrilla warfare in Ireland's fight for freedom. The 'False Surrender' controversy, during the decisive Kilmichael ambush, is brought into sharp focus in this book, so also is the controversy regarding sectarianism during the 1920–22 period.

Brother Against Brother
Liam Deasy

Liam Deasy's moving and sensitive account of the Civil War, one of Ireland's greatest tragedies. He recalls the circumstances surrounding his much-criticised order appealing to his comrades to call off the Civil War – an order that saved the lives of hundreds of prisoners. He also recounts his involvement in the ambush at Béal na mBláth, in which his close friend Michael Collins met his death on 22 August 1922. This book gives a rare and profound insight into the brutal, suicidal war that set father against son and brother against brother.

Baptised In Blood
The Formation of the Cork Brigade of Irish Volunteers 1913–16
Gerry White & Brendan O'Shea

Baptised in Blood records the formation of the Cork Brigade of the Irish Volunteers during a turbulent time in national and local politics.